PENGUIN TWENTIETH-CENTURY CLASSICS

EDWIN ARLINGTON ROBINSON: SELECTED POEMS

Edwin Arlington Robinson (1869–1935) grew up in Gardiner, Maine, attended Harvard University, worked as a time checker in the New York subway, and won the Pulitzer Prize for poetry three times. The author of over eighteen books of lyric and narrative poetry as well as plays, Robinson remains one of the most quietly influential and memorable poets of twentieth-century America.

Robert Faggen is Associate Professor of Literature at Claremont McKenna College and the author of *Robert Frost and the Challenge of Darwin* (University of Michigan Press) and editor of *Striving Towards Being: The Letters of Thomas Merton and Czeslaw Milosz* (Farrar, Straus & Giroux).

EDWIN ARLINGTON ROBINSON

SELECTED POEMS

EDITED WITH AN INTRODUCTION BY
ROBERT FAGGEN

PENGUIN BOOKS

PENGUIN BOOKS
Published by the Penguin Group
Penguin Putnam Inc., 375 Hudson Street,
New York, New York 10014, U.S.A.
Penguin Books Ltd, 27 Wrights Lane,
London W8 5TZ, England
Penguin Books Australia Ltd, Ringwood,
Victoria, Australia
Penguin Books Canada Ltd, 10 Alcorn Avenue,
Toronto, Ontario, Canada M4V 3B2
Penguin Books (N.Z.) Ltd, 182–190 Wairau Road,
Auckland 10, New Zealand

Penguin Books Ltd, Registered Offices:
Harmondsworth, Middlesex, England

First published in Penguin Books 1997

LIBRARY OF CONGRESS CATALOGING IN PUBLICATION DATA
Robinson, Edwin Arlington, 1869–1935.
[Poems. Selections]
Edwin Arlington Robinson/Selected poems; edited with an
introduction by Robert Faggen.
p. cm.
Includes bibliographical references (p.   ).
ISBN 0 14 01.8988 2 (pbk.)
I. Faggen, Robert.   II. Title.
PS3535.025A6   1997
811'.52—dc21   97–13727

Printed in the United States of America
Set in Stempel Garamond
Designed by Michael Mendelsohn

CONTENTS

CONTENTS ix

INTRODUCTION

Edwin Arlington Robinson is one of America's greatest poets, a fact well known to those who appreciate the power of English meters and the skillful handling of a body of sound to illuminate and shadow character in surprising and even terrifying ways. Robinson's interest in drama rather than in *ecriture,* in the perception of character rather than in introspective voyaging, have left him unjustly neglected by contemporary critics and, more important, readers. And his popularity during his own lifetime seems also to have kept the profound suspicious. But Robinson's technical skill as well as his relentless quest to discover what lies beyond human masquerade have created a powerful body of poems. Before Ezra Pound trumpeted the mantra of modernism, "Make it new," Robinson pioneered and mastered, as Robert Frost said, the "old-fashioned way to be new," exacting subtle but all the more powerful effects from refining and refreshing the genius of traditional forms and meters.

Robinson's characters are among the most memorable in American literature, and his genius rested in an ability to uncover the royal suffering of individuals beneath the veneer of affability and the postures of insolence and irascibility. He found heroic dignity and tragic passion and ambition lurking in the shadows of America. Before Pound and T. S. Eliot took their dissatisfaction with turn-of-the-century American culture to Europe, Robinson was steadily eroding the control of the genteel tradition in American letters by moving into the remote and neglected regions of life in the American village. His achievement made the scene ripe for all variety of moderns through cultivation of a subtle anti-poetry, avoiding Vic-

torian pieties while working within traditional and publicly
available forms to suggest human fear in the face of agonizing
choices and constraints.

His achievement is all the more remarkable because many
of his most memorable dramatic revelations occur in sonnets
or in lyrics of only seven or eight stanzas. In the twentieth
century, only Frost and W. B. Yeats could match Robinson's
ability to invest the sonnet with so much drama. He suggests
realms of grief, sorrow, and passion in crafted, formal verse
that defines the boundaries of what can and cannot be said
about another human being. His silences and sense of irony
tell much more than longer narratives, and he truly fulfilled
what he wrote in one of his later sonnets, "The Sheaves"—
the ideal of conveying "a mighty meaning of a kind / That tells
the more the more it is not told."

"Richard Cory" remains one of the most famous of these
characters, probably too famous because of the memorable,
violent irony of the poem. A man of royal bearing, he appears
to the uncomprehending narrator, a collective "we," enviable
for his wealth. But their perception of him reveals the limi-
tations of their standards of judgment. It is often the case in
Robinson that the narrators represent the collective and
democratizing society of the village, uneasy about the ambig-
uous difference they sense in these strange and often ex-
traordinary individuals. This tension in perception of others
at once better and worse goes to the heart of American pastoral
literature and its anxieties about equality. Cory's superiority
rests in something beyond material wealth but is a grief that
leads to suicide. What is wrong with him? Perhaps we should
not ask any more than we should ask what is wrong with
Herman Melville's Bartleby or J. D. Salinger's Seymour Glass,
except to say that these characters are painfully out of joint
with the society in which they live and carry within them a
tragic sense of the world's spiritual mediocrity. If in the words
of Melville's lawyer in "Bartleby," "misery hides aloof,"

many of Robinson's best characters—Reuben Bright, Miniver
Cheevy, Richard Cory, Flammonde, the woman of "The
Poor Relation," Eben Flood of "Mr. Flood's Party," and the
historical figures John Brown and Rembrandt—harbor de-
mons and passions in conflict with the world's indifference,
mediocrity, and cruelty. For Robinson presents a complex
and ambiguous figure in American thought: the aristocrat
castaway, or, as he says of Flammonde, "the Prince of Cast-
aways," someone who comes from anywhere and any occu-
pation but whose sometimes comic pride and blindness leads
him to a lonely and sometimes nearly mad existence apart
from society. Like Melville before him, Robinson was always
acutely aware of his characters' masks—the roles they chose
to play and the ones imposed upon them by society. In
"Flammonde," Robinson both suggests that his character is
only playing and also implies that there may have been some-
thing real beneath the mask:

> He never told us what he was,
> Or what mischance, or other cause,
> Had banished him from better days
> To play the Prince of Castaways.
> Meanwhile he played surpassing well
> A part, for most, unplayable;
> In fine, one pauses, half afraid
> To say for certain that he played.

Part of the fear generated in Robinson is the inability "to say
for certain" what causes a man or woman to be the way they
are; every bit of light in Robinson comes with commensu-
rate shadow, with speculation about "What small satanic sort
of kink/Was in his brain? What broken link/Withheld him
from the destinies/That came so near to being his?" Robinson
loved great failures, those who from their own crippling de-
mons dwelled in unfulfilled possibility.

Robinson's characters are often given both depth and humor by the distance of the narrator. In a masterpiece, "Mr. Flood's Party," Flood seems possessed of the "cryptic mirth" Robinson also ascribes to Lincoln but also represents another version of a "loon who cannot see that he is dead / Before God lets him die," as Rembrandt says to himself in "Rembrandt to Rembrandt." A would-be poet who knows "The Rubaiyat" and the "Song of Roland," Eben Flood (whose name suggests both the "ebb and flow" of a fluid and wavering character as well as a figure facing annihilation) responds to his life stripped of friends by singing, but only to a phantom of himself, alone, on the edge of nothingness, his vessel of futurity filled with drink. Like Richard Cory or Miniver Cheevy, the distance we feel from the characters—though it is different in each case—may be equal to the distance they feel from themselves, an ironic detachment that allows them greater dignity than their pathetic or tragic lives would allow.

Too much has been said of Robinson's sympathy for the common man, but this is not accurate. Rather, his affection is for the unnoticed, uncommon man and woman, suffering but determined to keep their power through both laughter and detachment in a cruel, spiritually belittered world. These include the Wandering Jew, Isaac and Archibald, and the woman of "The Poor Relation." Walt Whitman comes closer to an embracing affection for all individuals in the operatic, panoramic, and sometimes bumptiously egoistical sweep of his lines. But when reading Whitman, one always comes back to Whitman, a very complex persona who often conceals aspects of himself, his "real self," the "not me," within his gestures of openness. Robinson's brilliant concealment is of a different kind, in that he rarely opens himself up to our scrutiny except obliquely through the characters he portrays. Robinson has little of the concern with the "self" or with "subjectivity." While certainly we detect Robinson's woes and triumphs lurking behind the figures he offers, particularly in the later narrative poems, he does not invite us into a private psychological torment. Though the glimpses he gives us into his characters' psychology are often acute, Robinson's world is largely pre-Freudian in its speculative limits. Given what time has taught us of Freud, that might be a very good thing.

Robinson's life was his art, and he lived a near-hermit's existence—in New York City—even at the height of his fame. The facts of his childhood do not explain his isolation but certainly make it seem less surprising. He was born December 22, 1869, in the tiny village of Head Tide, Maine, the third son of Edward and Mary Robinson. His father, an entrepreneur, moved the family to the small, bleak town of Gardiner, Maine, which became the Tilbury Town of Robinson's poems. Herman, the oldest brother, lost most of the family money in the Panic of 1893 and eventually died of alcoholism, as did his father. Dean, the next oldest brother and a doctor, became addicted to morphine and eventually died of an overdose. Edwin, "Win" as his family called him, suffered a severely damaged ear from a blow given to him by a high school teacher, but it did little to damage his poetic gift. In 1890 he wrote, "I finally realized that I was doomed, or elected, or sentenced for life, to the writing of poetry. . . . I kept the grisly secret to myself," a comment that says much about the way his family and society regarded such a vocation for a promising young man as well as about the ambivalence with which Robinson regarded his own gift and ambition. His genius was recognized early by Laura E. Richards (1850–1943), a Pulitzer Prize–winning author who came to live in Gardiner and encouraged Robinson to study at Harvard. She once described him as "a slender figure, erect, distinguished, breeding and race in every line of it; dark, glowing eyes; brilliant color." At Harvard, Robinson continued to be a voracious reader but not a particularly devoted student. Though he studied literature, philosophy, and languages, his own inner calling was a greater preoccupation. Nevertheless, he was present during the golden age of Harvard philosophy, and he witnessed the ongoing debate between the idealism of Josiah Royce and the pragmatism of William James, as the two philosophers attempted to justify human life in an age claimed by scientism and materialism that found their culmination in various incarnations of Darwinism. Robinson was not a philosophical poet, but the question of the role of the imagination in transcending the material world figures prominently in his work and surfaces explicitly in "The Man Against the Sky" or the book *The Man Who Died Twice*. After a brief stint as an assistant to a Harvard dean, Robinson moved to New York. He lived a hermit's existence in a cosmopolitan world, devoting all of his available time to the craft of poetry and spending what little money he had available on concerts and opera. Despite reports of various affairs and love interests, including a proposal from Isadora Duncan, Robinson remained married only to his art.

Robinson's ambition and great confidence in his talent remained undaunted by the fact that he could not get his work published by literary journals and magazines. In 1896 he published his first book, *The Torrent and the Night Before*, at his own expense ($52), and a year later *The Children of the Night*. The people to whom he sent copies generally praised his efforts, and he took a job as a subway time checker to earn the living he could not from his life in verse. Though early notices of Robinson's work definitely noted his great ability, his intransigent solitude and financial predicament became notorious. In an article entitled "The Poet in the Subway," Joseph Lewis French described Robinson as "a mystery even to his friends. Though many have sought his acquaintance and his friendship he has preferred the lonely life here in New York as elsewhere. Those who have tried to lionize him as a new star on the literary horizon have all encountered this insurmountable obstacle. Those who have sought to befriend him in his hard struggle with the material facts of life have fared little better." But as Robinson wrote in the sonnet "Dear Friends": "So, friends (dear friends), remember, if you will,/The shame I win for singing is all mine,/The gold I miss for dreaming is all yours." Clearly he chose the integrity and perfection of his work over any kind of success in a culture he considered corrupt with money.

Robinson's pride was crippling, and his work in the subway consumed and depressed him. The years 1902 to 1904 found the poet suicidal and indulging deeply in drink. Then spectacular good fortune came to him from, of all places, the White House. Kermit Roosevelt, Theodore's son, read some of Robinson's work at Groton, the exclusive New England preparatory school, and sent a copy of *The Children of the Night* to the White House. The president was immediately impressed and told Richard Watson Gilder, the prominent New York literary editor, that he wanted to give Robinson a government post of the sort that had been given to Whitman and John Burroughs. Roosevelt is reported to have once stopped a meeting to ask a member of his Cabinet whether he had read Robinson. When the reply came back negative, Roosevelt ordered the statesman to spend the rest of the session reading *Captain Craig* aloud. On August 12, 1905, *Century* magazine contained a two-page review of *The Children of the Night* written by TR himself. Certainly, the endorsement of the president of the United States can be a mixed blessing, and Robinson suffered a bit from politically motivated critics attacking Roosevelt's taste and his intelligence. Nevertheless, Robinson did get a sinecure as a customs inspector, which at least freed him temporarily from the immense financial insecurity and distractions of his earlier employment.

Robinson's best books, all collections of short lyrics, followed *Captain Craig* (1905) in steady succession: *The Town Down the River* (1910), *The Man Against the Sky* (1916), *The Three Taverns* (1920), and *Avon's Harvest* (1921). Macmillan issued his *Collected Poems* in 1921, and the book received the first of Robinson's three Pulitzer Prizes. *Dionysus in Doubt* (1925) is driven by an undercurrent of attack on secular, puritanical America and the Eighteenth Amendment in particular, but it also contains some of Robinson's finest sonnets, particularly "The Sheaves" and "New England." The emergence of a new literary culture in America in the years just prior to World War I, one that was ready to accept the innovations of Frost, Eliot, and Pound, also found a place for Robinson's own idiosyncratic rebuke to turn-of-the-century literary gentility. By the time of his death on April 6, 1935, Robinson was one of the most venerated poets in America and had produced a collected opus of over 1,500 pages—all of it verse or dramatic verse. He never indulged in efforts of the left hand—neither fiction nor essays.

Robinson's development benefited greatly from his spending his summers from 1911 at the MacDowell Colony in Peterborough, New Hampshire. This artists' colony provided him with something of a sanctuary, though we can see from "Hillcrest," dedicated to Mrs. Edward MacDowell, that the utopian serenity of the place did not fail to produce in Robinson his characteristic uneasiness and uncertainty. The late Joseph Brodsky, who admired Robinson's work greatly and had planned to contribute a preface to this volume, saw in both Robinson and Frost an ability to create a sense of "controlled uncertainty" and a terror greater than that of tragedy because of its lack of resolution. In "Hillcrest," a series of quatrains contain conditional sentences about the possible benefits of contemplation, yet every assertion of revelation and resolution is tempered by a tentative sense of limited possibility:

> If here he venture to unroll
> His index of adagios,

And he be given to console
Humanity with what he knows,—

He may by contemplation learn
A little more than what he knew,
And even see great oaks return
To acorns out of which they grew.

He may, if he but listen well,
Through twilight and the silence here,
Be told what there are none may tell
To vanity's impatient ear;

And he may never dare again
Say what awaits him, or be sure
What sunlit labyrinth of pain
He may not enter and endure.

Contemplation and meditation lead to an undoing of prophetic, apocalyptic certainty and a consciousness only of the slow growth, death, and renewal of the tree of life and of knowledge, signified by the cycles of the "great oaks." The poem ends with a figure of one who recognizes that "all his wisdom is unfound" through the barely audible weaving of the mind in contemplation. Robinson has a genius for making rather dangerously abstract expressions of thought convincing because one can hear the creation and dissolution of closure in the controlled rhythms and rhymes of the lines rather than in startling or jarring images.

Robinson has always been a poet's poet, one for whom craft combined with insight into character forms the core of his achievement. But it is unfortunate that he has often been lumped in with the genteel tradition in American poetry, and this is very odd because he was really the pioneer who shattered genteel tastes. Robinson's is a world of tragedy, failure, unhappiness, one he deliberately crafted to shun gentility,

particularly as it manifested itself in the literary circles of New
York City. And Robinson also gave great expression to the
drama of the artist attempting to find a place for the imagi-
nation in a world dominated by crass capitalism, scientism,
and populism. If his style had an enormous influence on
Frost, John Crowe Ransom, and John Berryman, his ethos
was in league with the concerns of Eliot and Wallace Stevens.
Equally contemptuous of both capitalist and socialist ideals,
Robinson saw salvation in the labor and play of the imagi-
nation. The problem for Robinson, I believe, troubled the
greats who followed him: What value can or does the imag-
ination have in a world of eviscerated and sentimental reli-
gion? A review of his first book in 1897 complained of
Robinson's grimness: "There is true fire in his verse and there
are the swing and singing of wind and wave and the passion
of human emotion in his lines but limitations are vital. His
humor is of a grim sort and the world is not beautiful to him
but a prison house." Robinson's response revealed his con-
tempt for any facile connection to be made between beauty,
truth, and God: "I am sorry to learn that I have painted my-
self in such lugubrious colors. The world is not a 'prison
house,' but a kind of spiritual kindergarten where millions of
bewildered infants are trying to spell 'God' with the wrong
blocks." Robinson tells us as much about his audience as he
does about his own characters.

We can see a clear difference between Robinson and his
genteel and sentimental contemporaries if we compare him
with Richard Watson Gilder (1844–1909). Gilder along with
Edmund Clarence Stedman (1833–1908) and Richard Henry
Stoddard (1825–1903) were all major forces in the New York
literary scene, but to be fair they all gave Robinson their sup-
port. Stedman published five of Robinson's poems in *An
American Anthology, 1787–1900*, and Gilder, editor of the
Century, was instrumental in facilitating Robinson's associa-

tion with Roosevelt. Gilder's praise of great poets in "The Master Poets" is the kind of lyricism that will readily come out in the wash—stilted phrasing and puffy diction to fill out the lines that jingle with jangling rhymes and sanctimonious sentimentality:

> He the great World-Musician at whose stroke
> The stars of morning into music broke;
> He from whose Being Infinite are caught
> All harmonies of light, and sound, and thought—
> Once in each age, to keep the world in tune,
> He strikes a note sublime. Nor late, nor soon,
> A godlike soul,—music and passion's birth,—
> Vibrates across the discord of the earth
>   And sets the world aright.
>
>   O, these are they
> Who on men's hearts with mightiest power can play—
> The master poets of humanity,
> From heaven sent down to lift men to the sky.

Whoever these poets were, are, or will be, Gilder certainly was not one of them. But consider Robinson's praise of English poet George Crabbe (1754–1832) in his first book, *The Children of the Night*, in a poem that lacks all the ethereal bombast and stilted syntax of Gilder's effort. It immediately and dramatically engages and challenges the reader:

> Give him the darkest inch your shelf allows,
> Hide him in lonely garrets, if you will,—
> But his hard, human pulse is throbbing still
> With the sure strength that fearless truth endows.
> In spite of all fine science disavows,
> Of his plain excellence and stubborn skill,
> There yet remains what fashion cannot kill,
> Though years have thinned the laurel from his brows.

The octave of this sonnet gives dramatic embodiment to an ideal of poetry and a poet, one who though little read still maintained his own way against fashion by an objective attention to others, which Robinson's poem does in turn, and by clear, definite language. There is an easy confluence between the man and the book, but we still see the man in his stoical stubbornness. The rhymes of "will" and "still" and "skill" and "kill" emphasize the poet's strength and ability to survive and are not merely accidental ornaments.

Particularly striking is Robinson's ethical engagement with his audience, inviting them to consider Crabbe's "stubborn skill" while also insisting that the same skill stands in rebuke to the kind of misguided piety that praises "the flicker, not the flame":

> Whether or not we read him, we can feel
> From time to time the vigor of his name
> Against us like a finger for the shame
> And emptiness of what our souls reveal
> In books that are as altars where we kneel
> To consecrate the flicker, not the flame.

All the high-blown rhetoric about immortality we find in Gilder pales before the integrity, precision, and vigor—and, therefore, humility—we find in the less celebrated Crabbe and, as he would like his audience to know, in Robinson himself. Even when approaching the dreaded finger wag or moral, Robinson delivers it with great dramatic and metric force and, above all, wit. The sentence that forms the sestet drives forward and winds down with a forceful, yet balanced denouement, one at once concrete and dramatic as well as playful and suggestive.

Robinson wanted the public to recognize craft in the service of exposing the power of life in all walks rather than in grandstanding work of the would-be sage, as we can find not only in Gilder but in the more politically minded verse of

Robinson's venerable friend William Vaughn Moody. Robinson's subtlety in creating and sustaining interest in a character is in great evidence in "Reuben Bright." The poem goes far beyond, revealing that a butcher suffers deep emotional pain. It dramatizes an expression of grief unexpected from a man and no doubt surprising in its poignancy and violence to a feminized parlor-room audience that assumed such grief was for women only. Robinson's unabashed dig at the typical audience for poetry is dramatic, conveyed through the force of Bright's crying and the effect it has on the women around him. The poet's use of the monosyllable "shook" portrays with great concision the dramatic ferocity of the butcher's emotions, as does the simile "like a great baby" to describe both his innocence and his lack of control. But the real power is where it should be—in the denouement of the sestet. What will a butcher do now? What is he really about when the audience is gone? The violence that the butcher once invested in his profession reveals itself with terrifying irony in the private rituals of his grief, in the tearing down of the slaughterhouse:

> And after she was dead, and he had paid
> The singers and the sexton and the rest,
> He packed a lot of things that she had made
> Most mournfully away in an old chest
> Of hers, and put some chopped-up cedar boughs
> In with them, and tore down the slaughter house.

A certain eeriness attends to this strange and volatile conclusion. Robinson allows the conjunctions in the penultimate lines to build to the finale, which feels uncertain because of the staccato rhythm of the final phrase "and tore down the slaughter house." Why did he do this? Could he no longer confront the mutilation of flesh? Or does "slaughter house" become a metaphor for his own home, in which both he and his wife at times suffered from the silences and coldness of emotions that could not be expressed?

Even the name Reuben Bright evokes some of the darker paradoxes of Robinson's characters. Like those of his biblical namesake, this Reuben's words and actions may have been designed to hide a deeper guilt. That darker torment and ruefulness may also be the path to grace and light or merely a form of vanity and self-deception. As Robinson wrote in "Many Are Called," "invocation sacred and profane" cannot bring the light of grace to any; rather, it is only upon "the patience of the dead" that "questing light" may fall, and fall unexpectedly:

> Only at unconjectured intervals,
> By will of him on whom no man may gaze,
> By word of him whose law no man has read,
> A questing light may rift the sullen walls,
> To cling where mostly its infrequent rays
> Fall golden on the patience of the dead.

"The Sheaves," one of Robinson's finest sonnets, gives us a sense of the power of this light, which occurs precisely at the moment of change, death, and transformation: "Where long the shadows of the wind had rolled,/Green wheat was yielding to the change assigned;/And as by some vast magic undivined/The world was turning slowly into gold." Despite the sadness of the place, the once green wheat, now dead but gold, radiates a fleeting beauty underscored in the poet's stunning concluding analogy:

> So in a land where all days are not fair,
> Fair days went on till on another day
> A thousand golden sheaves were lying there,
> Shining and still, but not for long to stay—
> As if a thousand girls with golden hair
> Might rise from where they slept and go away.

INTRODUCTION   xxv

Robinson never pushes the revelations of madness or pas-
sion in the private lives of Tilbury Town, the poetic eponym
for his hometown of Gardiner, to the extent that Sherwood
Anderson did in writing about the intoxicated perversity of
Winesburg, Ohio (1919). But Robinson also never allows us
to forget the loneliness and terror that exists behind the peace-
ful and genteel communities of small-town America. Two of
his very best and most influential poems, "Eros Turannos"
and "The Mill," depict the lives of quiet desperation that drive
people to tragic ends. "Eros Turannos" captures the conver-
gence of the passions of two desperate people—a fortune-
seeker pursuing a wealthy old woman who would rather not
spend the rest of her years alone yet understands the terrible
motives of her lover. Though neither actually speaks, the bal-
ladlike lyric fuses both of their perspectives and the speaker's
own ironic distance. The poem reveals some of Robinson's
poetic debt as well as his influence. Critics from Yvor Winters
to Edwin Fussell have observed correctly that Robinson's
poetic precursors were largely English and not Ameri-
can—Wordsworth, Kipling, A. E. Housman, and particularly
Hardy. The pastoral influence of Wordsworth is present in
"Isaac and Archibald," but Robinson takes and perfects the
short ballads of Hardy and the fine elegies of Housman. The
sense of working within form gives power and shape to hu-
man drama. "Eros Turannos" begins with a woman possessed
by fear of a man whom she has chosen, and the monosyllables
of the opening phrase strike stark intensity. The tension be-
tween her choice and the tyranny of passion finds embodi-
ment in the first lines of the stanza before the downward drive
of the final four. Robinson makes one of the most brilliant
uses of rhyme in the language; the *abab* with which each
stanza begins finishes with the drive of the *cccb* as the re-
peating feminine rhyme "him" reverberates and envelopes her
thought and her choice with her fate: "choose him," "refuse
him," "lose him"; "sound him," "found him," "around him":

> She fears him, and will always ask
>   What fated her to choose him;
> She meets in his engaging mask
>   All reasons to refuse him;
> But what she meets and what she fears
> Are less than are the downward years,
> Drawn slowly to the foamless weirs
>   Of age, were she to lose him.

Thomas Hardy used the same eight-line stanza in "Wives in the Sere" as well as the repeated pronoun to emphasize the fate within choice, giving the short poem the effect of a ballad. But Hardy is less effective than Robinson because of the lack of variation and the awkwardness of a rhyming word such as "muser":

> Never a careworn wife but shows,
>   If a joy suffuse her,
> Something beautiful to those
>   Patient to peruse her,
> Some one charm the world unknows
>   Precious to a muser,
> Haply what, ere years were foes,
>   Moved her mate to choose her.

Robinson, the consummate craftsman, rarely resorts to the kind of awkard diction and syntax with which Hardy will, on occasion and with mixed success, fill up a line. But both clearly understood the power of form to complement the subject matter of a poem, and used the inevitable force of a rhymed stanza with far more control than the often overzealous Algernon Swinburne. Robert Frost learned much from Robinson's ability to evoke the unexpected within the constraints of form, and we can see it in such a lyric as "Reluctance" and in his sonnets. In Frost's "Paul's Wife," a narrative poem about the terrible fear and possessiveness of a husband, we have a moment that seems to echo both Hardy and Robinson:

> Paul was what's called a terrible possessor.
> Owning a wife with him meant owning her.
> She wasn't anybody else's business.
> Either to praise her, or so much as name her,
> And he'd thank people not to think of her.

Frost, one of Robinson's great admirers, once said that he was really like Robinson but with "the top button unbuttoned." Robinson himself was a pioneer in something Frost took further, namely, allowing the syntax and rhythms of ordinary speech to break across the strict regularity of meter, thereby maintaining the tension of a dramatic situation.

In both "Eros Turannos" and "The Unforgiven," men and women become slaves to the tyranny of love and both men and women can be shown to be cruel to one another as well as "blind" in their decisions. Within "Eros Turannos," Robinson reveals the blind passions and hidden fears of husband and wife in a swift and powerful shifting of perspectives that eventually converge in the third stanza:

> Between a blurred sagacity
>   That once had power to sound him,
> And Love, that will not let him be
>   The Judas that she found him,
> Her pride assuages her almost,
> As if it were alone the cost.—
> He sees that he will not be lost,
>   And waits and looks around him.
>
> A sense of ocean and old trees
>   Envelops and allures him;
> Tradition, touching all he sees,
>   Beguiles and reassures him;
> And all her doubts of what he says

Are dimmed with what she knows of days—
Till even prejudice delays
And fades, and she secures him.

Robinson allows each line to add a nuance to her hesitations
and justifications, and we see her suitor lying in wait as her
uncertainty about "what she knows of days" leads her to her
possession as she "secures him." A downward motion be-
comes the figure of tragedy in this poem as the location of
the house near the harbor reflects her fear of being "drawn
slowly to the foamless weirs/Of age." The line break under-
scores the psychological connection between drowning and
suicide and the inexorable power of time. Though Robinson's
imagination does not tend toward the mythic, especially in
his lyrics, the season does, of course, suggest the fall, and the
temptations of the tyrant god Eros in a lonely and isolated
world. Home, where her passion "lived and died," becomes
an asylum, in both senses of the word. All of Robinson's
characters suffer from the irony that almost any refuge and
any attempt to hide can never evade reality, a rending of mask
and veil. Yet, having taken us into the woman's blindness and
illusion, Robinson reminds us of the blindness and ignorance
of those in the town who "vibrate with her seclusion":

The falling leaf inaugurates
    The reign of her confusion;
The pounding wave reverberates
    The dirge of her illusion;
And home, where passion lived and died,
Becomes a place where she can hide,
While all the town and harbor side
    Vibrate with her seclusion.

Matters are even more desperate in "The Mill," a poem
whose title refers not only to what the husband does but to
life in the household, which has become a terrible and tragic

machinery of grief and suicide. The drama of the poem is terrifying because of the tension between the surface of facts and statements and their actual portent. We are confronted with a wife's slow realization that her husband's rather flat statement about the trial of the marketplace, "There are no millers any more," conceals in its simplicity depths of despair:

> The miller's wife had waited long,
>   The tea was cold, the fire was dead;
> And there might yet be nothing wrong
>   In how he went and what he said:
> "There are no millers any more,"
>   Was all that she had heard him say;
> And he had lingered at the door
>   So long that it seemed yesterday.

We are hardly privy to the miller's quiet desperation except through his wife's eventual grim discovery. The final stanza gives us a glimpse inside her soul as she, in a moment of intense grief after discovering her husband's hanging body, reasons and reasons because she suffers. The opacity of her own deliberations about his suicide matches the hidden desperation that her husband must have harbored before his death. She is drawn to the dark water in part because it "would leave no mark" but most important because such a death "would hide her." Robinson's tragic figures are often terribly driven by the pressures and sense of shame inflicted by the community:

> And if she thought it followed her,
>   She may have reasoned in the dark
> That one way of the few there were
>   Would hide her and would leave no mark:
> Black water, smooth above the weir
>   Like starry velvet in the night,

> Though ruffled once, would soon appear
> The same as ever to the sight.

The water becomes a metaphor for the way she wants to be perceived, "ruffled once" but eventually "the same as ever to the sight." But in painful irony this can happen only by suicide, by disappearing altogether from the sight of her neighbors into water reflecting the indifferent light of the stars.

Robinson had great contempt for the perceptions of a democratic mob that sought to understand and judge grief that was beyond its capacity. This remains the dominant theme of his superb portrait of Abraham Lincoln, "The Master," the title of which seeks to unveil the grandly tragic figure lurking behind the facade that a sentimental and misunderstanding nation has built around him. In "Demos," the personification of the spirit of democracy warns of the emergence of a demagogue from the shadows of populism and of the envy lurking beneath the veneer of egalitarianism. The warning given is clear: "See not the great among you for the small"; do not allow democracy to prevent the recognition of a natural aristocracy, distinguishing those truly suited to lead.

> So little have you seen of what awaits
>   Your fevered glimpse of a democracy
>   Confused and foiled with an equality
> Not equal to the envy it creates,
> That you see not how near you are the gates
>   Of an old king who listens fearfully
>   To you that are outside and are to be
> The noisy lords of imminent estates.

But Robinson could also handle his contempt as well as his morbid sense of belatedness with brilliance, as he did in the very fine "Miniver Cheevy." Each stanza contains two lines of contempt followed by two hilariously ironic undoings of his posture:

Miniver cursed the commonplace
   And eyed a khaki suit with loathing;
He missed the mediaeval grace
   Of iron clothing.

Miniver scorned the gold he sought,
   But sore annoyed was he without it;
Miniver thought, and thought, and thought,
   And thought about it.

The fourth "thought" is a little example of Robinson's genius for using form to set up expectations and then unsettle them with sharp humor.

Robinson's desire for a fit venue for his heroic visions did give way to some of his most ambitious and, for many critics, his least successful works—the long Arthurian narratives *Merlin* (1917), *Lancelot* (1920), and *Tristram* (1927). Though neglected for decades, *Tristram* was a best-seller (57,000 copies) and earned Robinson his third Pulitzer Prize. Merlin remains one of Robinson's most compelling visionaries, who despite the sadness of the situation and his age remains able to see future possibility by looking into himself. Both *Merlin* and *Tristram* contain hauntingly beautiful passages and are studies in a platonic and belated longing for a heroic sense of love and devotion beyond the ill fate of empire and national destruction. Their appearance during World War I and immediately after gives some insight into their inspiration and contemporary popularity. The poems that come after this achievement, the least known and discussed of the Robinson oeuvre, represent a pattern we have seen before in American literature—the artist desiring public success and shooting himself in the literary foot for pandering to the marketplace. For example, after the great success of his early novels, Herman Melville became increasingly disenchanted with the American publishing scene and the American public. To succeed in such a milieu was to fail by other and far greater standards. *Pierre* and later *Clarel* explore the questing and restless imagination in complete contempt of a bankrupt culture. If we look at *The Man Who Died Twice* (1924), which despite its grim dialogue garnered Robinson a second Pulitzer Prize, we encounter Fernando Nash, a once brilliant composer who subsequently burned his symphonies and then took up banging a drum in a sidewalk Salvation Army band and singing "Hallelujah" in the street. But he hears a new symphony in his head and, like the unwritten novel Melville's Pierre writes down in his heart, it is better than anything he had brought to the marketplace. Later in *Amaranth* (1934), we find the artist Fargo, who has burned his paintings and experiences a wild, infernal, and eventually purgatorial journey through which he comes around to accepting life in the real world. These poems deserve much closer attention if we are to understand the longings of the imagination in a desiccated world, the same longings that produced Eliot's *The Wasteland* and Stevens's *The Comedian as the Letter C*, to which Robinson's earlier long poem "Captain Craig" is indebted. Robinson pioneered the modern long poem of the ironic and existential artist attempting to create light in the dark. He portrays well what Robert Browning did, the cranky, failed artist and the would-be titan who lives in a world that cannot tell fakes from the real thing and whose personal torments are at least as interesting as his art. Sympathetic and ironic, Robinson always seeks the truth, however sad, behind the masks and apparent madness of his visionary characters. If he is not as successful as Browning, it is because he does not let his characters speak enough for themselves through the fascinating, terse, and sometimes extravagant indirections that made the Victorian's monologues so powerful.

In the present volume, in which only Robinson's shorter poems are represented, we do have the remarkable and successful dramatic monologue "Rembrandt to Rembrandt," a self-portrait of the artist who sees his greatest work behind him and must learn to accept his demons and his passions beyond the cravings of the marketplace and within the darkness of his own imaginative prison. Here, the Dutch painter speaks not to a living person or precisely to himself but to a self-portrait of himself painted years earlier. It is, then, a self-portrait within a self-portrait, saturnine and deeply expressive of the artist's resolution to go on with his work despite the loss of his wife, the abandonment by his community, and an attachment to only his own isolated imagination. Robinson builds the meditation in gradual movements with subtle figures. Haunted by voices of assurance of doubt and regarding himself as "a living instrument/Played on by powers that are invisible," the painter wonders whether he should produce more but without the depth and quality that he feels compelled to create. But Apollo tells him to follow his own demon, and his demon is surely a disturbing and guiding light:

> Your Dutchmen, who are swearing at you still
> For your pernicious filching of their florins,
> May likely curse you down their generation,
> Not having understood there was no malice
> Or grinning evil in a golden shadow
> That shall outshine their slight identities
> And hold their faces when their names are nothing.
> But this, as you discern, or should by now
> Surmise, for you is neither here nor there:
> You made your picture as your demon willed it;
> That's about all of that. Now make as many
> As may be to be made,—for so you will,
> Whatever the toll may be, and hold your light
> So that you see, without so much to blind you
> As even the cobweb-flash of a misgiving,
> Assured and certain that if you see right

> Others will have to see—albeit their seeing
> Shall irk them out of their serenity
> For such a time as umbrage may require.

Vision and light become the dominant themes of Robinson's later work, an Emersonian sense of commitment to one's own vision despite the demands of the marketplace. Despite the loneliness, Rembrandt accepted living only by his "widowed gold," his light born of the experience of terrible loss. All the welcome he hopes for will remain unfulfilled, and the poem ends with exquisite acceptance of being "anchored" in the darkness:

> . . . If at the first
> Of your long turning, which may still be longer
> Than even your faith has measured it, you sigh
> For distant welcome that may not be seen,
> Or wayside shouting that will not be heard,
> You may as well accommodate your greatness
> To the convenience of an easy ditch,
> And, anchored there with all your widowed gold,
> Forget your darkness in the dark, and hear
> No longer the cold wash of Holland scorn.

It is a powerful drama of a soul in need of love and fame and all the while fearing that kind of success as compromise. Robinson's heroes are always seekers of the light, the dominant spiritual figure in his work. Robinson accepted the world as it is and yet always placed greatest value on those able to see beyond it (he once said that "the world is a hell of a place, but the universe is a fine thing"), driven by an inner demonic fire into a purifying vision. He once wrote, "The age is all right, material progress is all right, Herbert Spencer is all right, hell is all right. These things are temporal necessities, but they are damned uninteresting to one who could get a glimpse of the real light through the clouds of time." Or, as

Robinson's Saint Paul says in "The Three Taverns": "The
best of life, until we see beyond/The shadows of ourselves
(and they are less/Than even the blindest of indignant eyes/
Would have them) is in what we do not know." Robinson
always sought the best of life and the unknown through the
darkest of his and our own shadows.

SUGGESTIONS FOR FURTHER READING

Barnard, Ellsworth. *Edwin Arlington Robinson: A Critical Study*. New York: Macmillan, 1952.

———, ed. *Edwin Arlington Robinson: Centenary Essays*. Athens: The University of Georgia Press, 1969.

Donoghue, Denis. *Connoisseurs of Chaos*. New York: Columbia University Press, 1984.

Frost, Robert. Introduction to *King Jasper* by Edwin Arlington Robinson. New York: Macmillan, 1935. Reprinted in *Robert Frost: Collected Poems, Plays, and Prose*, Richard Poirier and Mark Edmundson, eds. New York: Library of America, 1995.

Fussell, Edwin Sill. *Philosophy in the Poetry of Edwin Arlington Robinson*. Berkeley: University of California Press, 1954.

Hagerdon, Herman. *Edwin Arlington Robinson*. New York: Macmillan, 1939.

Murphy, Francis, ed. *Edwin Arlington Robinson: A Collection of Critical Essays*. Englewood Cliffs, N.J.: Prentice Hall, 1970.

Neff, Emery. *Edwin Arlington Robinson*. New York: Sloan, 1948.

Robinson, Edwin Arlington. *Collected Poems*. New York: Macmillan, 1937.

———. *Selected Letters*. Introduction by Ridgely Torrence. New York: Macmillan, 1940.

———. *Untriangulated Stars: Letters of Edwin Arlington Robinson to Harry de Forest Smith: 1890–1905*, Denham Sutcliffe, ed. Cambridge, Mass.: Harvard University Press, 1947.

Waggoner, Hyatt Howe. "E. A. Robinson and the Cosmic Chill," *New England Quarterly* XIII (1940), 65–84.

Winters, Ivor. *Edwin Arlington Robinson*. New York: New Directions, 1946.

A NOTE ON THE TEXTS

The poems in this volume have all been taken from the *Collected Poems* of Edwin Arlington Robinson published by The Macmillan Company, New York, first in 1921 and later, in a "complete edition with additional poems," in 1937. The text follows the edition of 1937 in its twelfth printing, 1959.

SELECTED POEMS

JOHN EVERELDOWN

"Where are you going to-night, to-night,—
   Where are you going, John Evereldown?
There's never the sign of a star in sight,
   Nor a lamp that's nearer than Tilbury Town.
5 Why do you stare as a dead man might?
Where are you pointing away from the light?
And where are you going to-night, to-night,—
   Where are you going, John Evereldown?"

"Right through the forest, where none can see,
10   There's where I'm going, to Tilbury Town.
The men are asleep,—or awake, may be,—
   But the women are calling John Evereldown.
Ever and ever they call for me,
And while they call can a man be free?
15 So right through the forest, where none can see,
   There's where I'm going, to Tilbury Town."

"But why are you going so late, so late,—
   Why are you going, John Evereldown?
Though the road be smooth and the way be straight,
20   There are two long leagues to Tilbury Town.
Come in by the fire, old man, and wait!
Why do you chatter out there by the gate?
And why are you going so late, so late,—
   Why are you going, John Evereldown?"

25　"I follow the women wherever they call,—
　　　That's why I'm going to Tilbury Town.
　　God knows if I pray to be done with it all,
　　　But God is no friend to John Evereldown.
　　So the clouds may come and the rain may fall,
30　The shadows may creep and the dead men crawl,—
　　But I follow the women wherever they call,
　　　And that's why I'm going to Tilbury Town."

LUKE HAVERGAL

Go to the western gate, Luke Havergal,
There where the vines cling crimson on the wall,
And in the twilight wait for what will come.
The leaves will whisper there of her, and some,
Like flying words, will strike you as they fall;
But go, and if you listen she will call.
Go to the western gate, Luke Havergal—
Luke Havergal.

No, there is not a dawn in eastern skies
To rift the fiery night that's in your eyes;
But there, where western glooms are gathering,
The dark will end the dark, if anything:
God slays Himself with every leaf that flies,
And hell is more than half of paradise.
No, there is not a dawn in eastern skies—
In eastern skies.

Out of a grave I come to tell you this,
Out of a grave I come to quench the kiss
That flames upon your forehead with a glow
That blinds you to the way that you must go.
Yes, there is yet one way to where she is,
Bitter, but one that faith may never miss.
Out of a grave I come to tell you this—
To tell you this.

25 There is the western gate, Luke Havergal,
There are the crimson leaves upon the wall.
Go, for the winds are tearing them away,—
Nor think to riddle the dead words they say,
Nor any more to feel them as they fall;
30 But go, and if you trust her she will call.
There is the western gate, Luke Havergal—
Luke Havergal.

VILLANELLE OF CHANGE

Since Persia fell at Marathon,
 The yellow years have gathered fast:
Long centuries have come and gone.

And yet (they say) the place will don
 A phantom fury of the past,
Since Persia fell at Marathon;

And as of old, when Helicon
 Trembled and swayed with rapture vast
(Long centuries have come and gone),

This ancient plain, when night comes on,
 Shakes to a ghostly battle-blast,
Since Persia fell at Marathon.

But into soundless Acheron
 The glory of Greek shame was cast:
Long centuries have come and gone,

The suns of Hellas have all shone,
 The first has fallen to the last:—
Since Persia fell at Marathon,
Long centuries have come and gone.

THE HOUSE ON THE HILL

They are all gone away,
   The House is shut and still,
There is nothing more to say.

Through broken walls and gray
5   The winds blow bleak and shrill:
They are all gone away.

Nor is there one to-day
   To speak them good or ill:
There is nothing more to say.

10 Why is it then we stray
   Around the sunken sill?
They are all gone away,

And our poor fancy-play
   For them is wasted skill:
15 There is nothing more to say.

There is ruin and decay
   In the House on the Hill:
They are all gone away,
There is nothing more to say.

RICHARD CORY

Whenever Richard Cory went down town,
We people on the pavement looked at him:
He was a gentleman from sole to crown,
Clean favored, and imperially slim.

5   And he was always quietly arrayed,
And he was always human when he talked;
But still he fluttered pulses when he said,
"Good-morning," and he glittered when he walked.

And he was rich—yes, richer than a king—
10   And admirably schooled in every grace:
In fine, we thought that he was everything
To make us wish that we were in his place.

So on we worked, and waited for the light,
And went without the meat, and cursed the bread;
15   And Richard Cory, one calm summer night,
Went home and put a bullet through his head.

CALVARY

Friendless and faint, with martyred steps and slow,
Faint for the flesh, but for the spirit free,
Stung by the mob that came to see the show,
The Master toiled along to Calvary;
5   We gibed him, as he went, with houndish glee,
Till his dimmed eyes for us did overflow;
We cursed his vengeless hands thrice wretchedly,—
And this was nineteen hundred years ago.

But after nineteen hundred years the shame
10   Still clings, and we have not made good the loss
That outraged faith has entered in his name.
Ah, when shall come love's courage to be strong!
Tell me, O Lord—tell me, O Lord, how long
Are we to keep Christ writhing on the cross!

DEAR FRIENDS

Dear friends, reproach me not for what I do,
Nor counsel me, nor pity me; nor say
That I am wearing half my life away
For bubble-work that only fools pursue.
And if my bubbles be too small for you,
Blow bigger then your own: the games we play
To fill the frittered minutes of a day,
Good glasses are to read the spirit through.

And whoso reads may get him some shrewd skill;
And some unprofitable scorn resign,
To praise the very thing that he deplores;
So, friends (dear friends), remember, if you will,
The shame I win for singing is all mine,
The gold I miss for dreaming is all yours.

THE STORY OF THE ASHES
AND THE FLAME

No matter why, nor whence, nor when she came,
There was her place. No matter what men said,
No matter what she was; living or dead,
Faithful or not, he loved her all the same.
5   The story was as old as human shame,
But ever since that lonely night she fled,
With books to blind him, he had only read
The story of the ashes and the flame.

There she was always coming pretty soon
10   To fool him back, with penitent scared eyes
That had in them the laughter of the moon
For baffled lovers, and to make him think—
Before she gave him time enough to wink—
Her kisses were the keys to Paradise.

AMARYLLIS

Once, when I wandered in the woods alone,
An old man tottered up to me and said,
"Come, friend, and see the grave that I have made
For Amaryllis." There was in the tone
5   Of his complaint such quaver and such moan
That I took pity on him and obeyed,
And long stood looking where his hands had laid
An ancient woman, shrunk to skin and bone.

Far out beyond the forest I could hear
10 The calling of loud progress, and the bold
Incessant scream of commerce ringing clear;
But though the trumpets of the world were glad,
It made me lonely and it made me sad
To think that Amaryllis had grown old.

ZOLA

Because he puts the compromising chart
Of hell before your eyes, you are afraid;
Because he counts the price that you have paid
For innocence, and counts it from the start,
5   You loathe him. But he sees the human heart
Of God meanwhile, and in His hand was weighed
Your squeamish and emasculate crusade
Against the grim dominion of his art.

Never until we conquer the uncouth
10   Connivings of our shamed indifference
(We call it Christian faith) are we to scan
The racked and shrieking hideousness of Truth
To find, in hate's polluted self-defence
Throbbing, the pulse, the divine heart of man.

THE PITY OF THE LEAVES

Vengeful across the cold November moors,
Loud with ancestral shame there came the bleak
Sad wind that shrieked, and answered with a shriek,
Reverberant through lonely corridors.
5   The old man heard it; and he heard, perforce,
Words out of lips that were no more to speak—
Words of the past that shook the old man's cheek
Like dead, remembered footsteps on old floors.

And then there were the leaves that plagued him so!
10   The brown, thin leaves that on the stones outside
Skipped with a freezing whisper. Now and then
They stopped, and stayed there—just to let him know
How dead they were, but if the old man cried,
They fluttered off like withered souls of men.

AARON STARK

Withal a meagre man was Aaron Stark,
Cursed and unkempt, shrewd, shrivelled, and morose.
A miser was he, with a miser's nose,
And eyes like little dollars in the dark.
His thin, pinched mouth was nothing but a mark;
And when he spoke there came like sullen blows
Through scattered fangs a few snarled words and
    close,
As if a cur were chary of its bark.

Glad for the murmur of his hard renown,
Year after year he shambled through the town,
A loveless exile moving with a staff;
And oftentimes there crept into his ears
A sound of alien pity, touched with tears,—
And then (and only then) did Aaron laugh.

THE GARDEN

There is a fenceless garden overgrown
With buds and blossoms and all sorts of leaves;
And once, among the roses and the sheaves,
The Gardener and I were there alone.
5 He led me to the plot where I had thrown
The fennel of my days on wasted ground,
And in that riot of sad weeds I found
The fruitage of a life that was my own.

My life! Ah, yes, there was my life, indeed!
10 And there were all the lives of humankind;
And they were like a book that I could read,
Whose every leaf, miraculously signed,
Outrolled itself from Thought's eternal seed.
Love-rooted in God's garden of the mind.

CLIFF KLINGENHAGEN

Cliff Klingenhagen had me in to dine
With him one day; and after soup and meat,
And all the other things there were to eat,
Cliff took two glasses and filled one with wine
5   And one with wormwood. Then, without a sign
For me to choose at all, he took the draught
Of bitterness himself, and lightly quaffed
It off, and said the other one was mine.

And when I asked him what the deuce he meant
10   By doing that, he only looked at me
And smiled, and said it was a way of his.
And though I know the fellow, I have spent
Long time a-wondering when I shall be
As happy as Cliff Klingenhagen is.

REUBEN BRIGHT

Because he was a butcher and thereby
Did earn an honest living (and did right),
I would not have you think that Reuben Bright
Was any more a brute than you or I;
5   For when they told him that his wife must die,
He stared at them, and shook with grief and fright,
And cried like a great baby half that night,
And made the women cry to see him cry.

And after she was dead, and he had paid
10 The singers and the sexton and the rest,
He packed a lot of things that she had made
Most mournfully away in an old chest
Of hers, and put some chopped-up cedar boughs
In with them, and tore down the slaughter house.

THE ALTAR

Alone, remote, nor witting where I went,
I found an altar builded in a dream—
A fiery place, whereof there was a gleam
So swift, so searching, and so eloquent
5   Of upward promise, that love's murmur, blent
With sorrow's warning, gave but a supreme
Unending impulse to that human stream
Whose flood was all for the flame's fury bent.

Alas! I said,—the world is in the wrong.
10   But the same quenchless fever of unrest
That thrilled the foremost of that martyred throng
Thrilled me, and I awoke . . . and was the same
Bewildered insect plunging for the flame
That burns, and must burn somehow for the best.

THE TAVERN

Whenever I go by there nowadays
And look at the rank weeds and the strange grass,
The torn blue curtains and the broken glass,
I seem to be afraid of the old place;
5   And something stiffens up and down my face,
For all the world as if I saw the ghost
Of old Ham Amory, the murdered host,
With his dead eyes turned on me all aglaze.

The Tavern has a story, but no man
10   Can tell us what it is. We only know
That once long after midnight, years ago,
A stranger galloped up from Tilbury Town,
Who brushed, and scared, and all but overran
That skirt-crazed reprobate, John Evereldown.

GEORGE CRABBE

Give him the darkest inch your shelf allows,
Hide him in lonely garrets, if you will,—
But his hard, human pulse is throbbing still
With the sure strength that fearless truth endows.
5   In spite of all fine science disavows,
Of his plain excellence and stubborn skill
There yet remains what fashion cannot kill,
Though years have thinned the laurel from his brows.

Whether or not we read him, we can feel
10   From time to time the vigor of his name
Against us like a finger for the shame
And emptiness of what our souls reveal
In books that are as altars where we kneel
To consecrate the flicker, not the flame.

CREDO

I cannot find my way: there is no star
In all the shrouded heavens anywhere;
And there is not a whisper in the air
Of any living voice but one so far
5   That I can hear it only as a bar
Of lost, imperial music, played when fair
And angel fingers wove, and unaware,
Dead leaves to garlands where no roses are.

No, there is not a glimmer, nor a call,
10 For one that welcomes, welcomes when he fears,
The black and awful chaos of the night;
For through it all—above, beyond it all—
I know the far-sent message of the years,
I feel the coming glory of the Light.

ON THE NIGHT OF A
FRIEND'S WEDDING

If ever I am old, and all alone,
I shall have killed one grief, at any rate;
For then, thank God, I shall not have to wait
Much longer for the sheaves that I have sown.
5 The devil only knows what I have done,
But here I am, and here are six or eight
Good friends, who most ingenuously prate
About my songs to such and such a one.

But everything is all askew to-night,—
10 As if the time were come, or almost come,
For their untenanted mirage of me
To lose itself and crumble out of sight,
Like a tall ship that floats above the foam
A little while, and then breaks utterly.

SONNET

The master and the slave go hand in hand,
Though touch be lost. The poet is a slave,
And there be kings do sorrowfully crave
The joyance that a scullion may command.
5   But, ah, the sonnet-slave must understand
The mission of his bondage, or the grave
May clasp his bones, or ever he shall save
The perfect word that is the poet's wand.

The sonnet is a crown, whereof the rhymes
10   Are for Thought's purest gold the jewel-stones;
But shapes and echoes that are never done
Will haunt the workshop, as regret sometimes
Will bring with human yearning to sad thrones
The crash of battles that are never won.

ISAAC AND ARCHIBALD

(To Mrs. Henry Richards)

Isaac and Archibald were two old men.
I knew them, and I may have laughed at them
A little; but I must have honored them
For they were old, and they were good to me.

5   I do not think of either of them now,
Without remembering, infallibly,
A journey that I made one afternoon
With Isaac to find out what Archibald
Was doing with his oats. It was high time
10 Those oats were cut, said Isaac; and he feared
That Archibald—well, he could never feel
Quite sure of Archibald. Accordingly
The good old man invited me—that is,
Permitted me—to go along with him;
15 And I, with a small boy's adhesiveness
To competent old age, got up and went.

I do not know that I cared overmuch
For Archibald's or anybody's oats,
But Archibald was quite another thing,
20 And Isaac yet another; and the world
Was wide, and there was gladness everywhere.
We walked together down the River Road
With all the warmth and wonder of the land
Around us, and the wayside flash of leaves,—
25 And Isaac said the day was glorious;
But somewhere at the end of the first mile

I found that I was figuring to find
How long those ancient legs of his would keep
The pace that he had set for them. The sun
30   Was hot, and I was ready to sweat blood;
But Isaac, for aught I could make of him,
Was cool to his hat-band. So I said then
With a dry gasp of affable despair,
Something about the scorching days we have
35   In August without knowing it sometimes;
But Isaac said the day was like a dream,
And praised the Lord, and talked about the breeze.
I made a fair confession of the breeze,
And crowded casually on his thought
40   The nearness of a profitable nook
That I could see. First I was half inclined
To caution him that he was growing old,
But something that was not compassion soon
Made plain the folly of all subterfuge.
45   Isaac was old, but not so old as that.

So I proposed, without an overture,
That we be seated in the shade a while,
And Isaac made no murmur. Soon the talk
Was turned on Archibald, and I began
50   To feel some premonitions of a kind
That only childhood knows; for the old man
Had looked at me and clutched me with his eye,
And asked if I had ever noticed things.
I told him that I could not think of them,
55   And I knew then, by the frown that left his face
Unsatisfied, that I had injured him.
"My good young friend," he said, "you cannot feel
What I have seen so long. You have the eyes—
Oh, yes—but you have not the other things:
60   The sight within that never will deceive,

27

You do not know—you have no right to know;
The twilight warning of experience,
The singular idea of loneliness,—
These are not yours. But they have long been mine,
65   And they have shown me now for seven years
That Archibald is changing. It is not
So much that he should come to his last hand,
And leave the game, and go the old way down;
But I have known him in and out so long,
70   And I have seen so much of good in him
That other men have shared and have not seen,
And I have gone so far through thick and thin,
Through cold and fire with him, that now it brings
To this old heart of mine an ache that you
75   Have not yet lived enough to know about.
But even unto you, and your boy's faith,
Your freedom, and your untried confidence,
A time will come to find out what it means
To know that you are losing what was yours,
80   To know that you are being left behind;
And then the long contempt of innocence—
God bless you, boy!—don't think the worse of it
Because an old man chatters in the shade—
Will all be like a story you have read
85   In childhood and remembered for the pictures.

And when the best friend of your life goes down,
When first you know in him the slackening
That comes, and coming always tells the end,—
Now in a common word that would have passed
90   Uncaught from any other lips than his,
Now in some trivial act of every day,
Done as he might have done it all along
But for a twinging little difference
That nips you like a squirrel's teeth—oh, yes,

28

95 Then you will understand it well enough.
  But oftener it comes in other ways;
  It comes without your knowing when it comes;
  You know that he is changing, and you know
  That he is going—just as I know now
100 That Archibald is going, and that I
  Am staying. . . . Look at me, my boy,
  And when the time shall come for you to see
  That I must follow after him, try then
  To think of me, to bring me back again,
105 Just as I was to-day. Think of the place
  Where we are sitting now, and think of me—
  Think of old Isaac as you knew him then,
  When you set out with him in August once
  To see old Archibald."—The words come back
110 Almost as Isaac must have uttered them,
  And there comes with them a dry memory
  Of something in my throat that would not move.

  If you had asked me then to tell just why
  I made so much of Isaac and the things
115 He said, I should have gone far for an answer;
  For I knew it was not sorrow that I felt,
  Whatever I may have wished it, or tried then
  To make myself believe. My mouth was full
  Of words, and they would have been comforting
120 To Isaac, spite of my twelve years, I think;
  But there was not in me the willingness
  To speak them out. Therefore I watched the ground;
  And I was wondering what made the Lord
  Create a thing so nervous as an ant,
125 When Isaac, with commendable unrest,
  Ordained that we should take the road again—
  For it was yet three miles to Archibald's,
  And one to the first pump. I felt relieved

All over when the old man told me that;
130   I felt that he had stilled a fear of mine
That those extremities of heat and cold
Which he had long gone through with Archibald
Had made the man impervious to both;
But Isaac had a desert somewhere in him,
135   And at the pump he thanked God for all things
That He had put on earth for men to drink,
And he drank well,—so well that I proposed
That we go slowly lest I learn too soon
The bitterness of being left behind,
140   And all those other things. That was a joke
To Isaac, and it pleased him very much;
And that pleased me—for I was twelve years old.

At the end of an hour's walking after that
The cottage of old Archibald appeared.
145   Little and white and high on a smooth round hill
It stood, with hackmatacks and apple-trees
Before it, and a big barn-roof beyond;
And over the place—trees, houses, fields and all—
Hovered an air of still simplicity
150   And a fragrance of old summers—the old style
That lives the while it passes. I dare say
That I was lightly conscious of all this
When Isaac, of a sudden, stopped himself,
And for the long first quarter of a minute
155   Gazed with incredulous eyes, forgetful quite
Of breezes and of me and of all else
Under the scorching sun but a smooth-cut field,
Faint yellow in the distance. I was young,
But there were a few things that I could see,
160   And this was one of them.—"Well, well!" said he;
And "Archibald will be surprised, I think,"
Said I. But all my childhood subtlety

Was lost on Isaac, for he strode along
Like something out of Homer—powerful
165 And awful on the wayside, so I thought.
Also I thought how good it was to be
So near the end of my short-legged endeavor
To keep the pace with Isaac for five miles.

Hardly had we turned in from the main road
170 When Archibald, with one hand on his back
And the other clutching his huge-headed cane,
Came limping down to meet us.—"Well! well! well!"
Said he; and then he looked at my red face,
All streaked with dust and sweat, and shook my hand,
175 And said it must have been a right smart walk
That we had had that day from Tilbury Town.—
"Magnificent," said Isaac; and he told
About the beautiful west wind there was
Which cooled and clarified the atmosphere.
180 "You must have made it with your legs, I guess,"
Said Archibald; and Isaac humored him
With one of those infrequent smiles of his
Which he kept in reserve, apparently,
For Archibald alone. "But why," said he,
185 "Should Providence have cider in the world
If not for such an afternoon as this?"
And Archibald, with a soft light in his eyes,
Replied that if he chose to go down cellar,
There he would find eight barrels—one of which
190 Was newly tapped, he said, and to his taste
An honor to the fruit. Isaac approved
Most heartily of that, and guided us
Forthwith, as if his venerable feet
Were measuring the turf in his own door-yard,
195 Straight to the open rollway. Down we went,
Out of the fiery sunshine to the gloom,

Grateful and half sepulchral, where we found
The barrels, like eight potent sentinels,
Close ranged along the wall. From one of them
200 A bright pine spile stuck out alluringly,
And on the black flat stone, just under it,
Glimmered a late-spilled proof that Archibald
Had spoken from unfeigned experience.
There was a fluted antique water-glass
205 Close by, and in it, prisoned, or at rest,
There was a cricket, of the brown soft sort
That feeds on darkness. Isaac turned him out,
And touched him with his thumb to make him jump,
And then composedly pulled out the plug
210 With such a practised hand that scarce a drop
Did even touch his fingers. Then he drank
And smacked his lips with a slow patronage
And looked along the line of barrels there
With a pride that may have been forgetfulness
215 That they were Archibald's and not his own.
"I never twist a spigot nowadays,"
He said, and raised the glass up to the light,
"But I thank God for orchards." And that glass
Was filled repeatedly for the same hand
220 Before I thought it worth while to discern
Again that I was young, and that old age,
With all his woes, had some advantages.

"Now, Archibald," said Isaac, when we stood
Outside again, "I have it in my mind
225 That I shall take a sort of little walk—
To stretch my legs and see what you are doing.
You stay and rest your back and tell the boy
A story: Tell him all about the time
In Stafford's cabin forty years ago,
230 When four of us were snowed up for ten days

32

With only one dried haddock. Tell him all
About it, and be wary of your back.
Now I will go along."—I looked up then
At Archibald, and as I looked I saw
235 Just how his nostrils widened once or twice
And then grew narrow. I can hear to-day
The way the old man chuckled to himself—
Not wholesomely, not wholly to convince
Another of his mirth,—as I can hear
240 The lonely sigh that followed.—But at length
He said: "The orchard now's the place for us;
We may find something like an apple there,
And we shall have the shade, at any rate."
So there we went and there we laid ourselves
245 Where the sun could not reach us; and I champed
A dozen of worm-blighted astrakhans
While Archibald said nothing—merely told
The tale of Stafford's cabin, which was good,
Though "master chilly"—after his own phrase—
250 Even for a day like that. But other thoughts
Were moving in his mind, imperative,
And writhing to be spoken: I could see
The glimmer of them in a glance or two,
Cautious, or else unconscious, that he gave
255 Over his shoulder: . . . "Stafford and the rest—
But that's an old song now, and Archibald
And Isaac are old men. Remember, boy,
That we are old. Whatever we have gained,
Or lost, or thrown away, we are old men.
260 You look before you and we look behind,
And we are playing life out in the shadow—
But that's not all of it. The sunshine lights
A good road yet before us if we look,
And we are doing that when least we know it;
265 For both of us are children of the sun,

33

Like you, and like the weed there at your feet.
The shadow calls us, and it frightens us—
We think; but there's a light behind the stars
And we old fellows who have dared to live,
270 We see it—and we see the other things,
The other things . . . Yes, I have seen it come
These eight years, and these ten years, and I know
Now that it cannot be for very long
That Isaac will be Isaac. You have seen—
275 Young as you are, you must have seen the strange
Uncomfortable habit of the man?
He'll take my nerves and tie them in a knot
Sometimes, and that's not Isaac. I know that—
And I know what it is: I get it here
280 A little, in my knees, and Isaac—here."
The old man shook his head regretfully
And laid his knuckles three times on his forehead.
"That's what it is: Isaac is not quite right.
You see it, but you don't know what it means:
285 The thousand little differences—no,
You do not know them, and it's well you don't;
You'll know them soon enough—God bless
       you, boy!—
You'll know them, but not all of them—not all.
So think of them as little as you can:
290 There's nothing in them for you, or for me—
But I am old and I must think of them;
I'm in the shadow, but I don't forget
The light, my boy,—the light behind the stars.
Remember that: remember that I said it;
295 And when the time that you think far away
Shall come for you to say it—say it, boy;
Let there be no confusion or distrust
In you, no snarling of a life half lived,
Nor any cursing over broken things

34

300 That your complaint has been the ruin of.
Live to see clearly and the light will come
To you, and as you need it.—But there, there,
I'm going it again, as Isaac says,
And I'll stop now before you go to sleep.—
305 Only be sure that you growl cautiously,
And always where the shadow may not reach you."

Never shall I forget, long as I live,
The quaint thin crack in Archibald's voice,
The lonely twinkle in his little eyes,
310 Or the way it made me feel to be with him.
I know I lay and looked for a long time
Down through the orchard and across the road,
Across the river and the sun-scorched hills
That ceased in a blue forest, where the world
315 Ceased with it. Now and then my fancy caught
A flying glimpse of a good life beyond—
Something of ships and sunlight, streets and singing,
Troy falling, and the ages coming back,
And ages coming forward: Archibald
320 And Isaac were good fellows in old clothes,
And Agamemnon was a friend of mine;
Ulysses coming home again to shoot
With bows and feathered arrows made another,
And all was as it should be. I was young.

325 So I lay dreaming of what things I would,
Calm and incorrigibly satisfied
With apples and romance and ignorance,
And the still smoke from Archibald's clay pipe.
There was a stillness over everything,
330 As if the spirit of heat had laid its hand
Upon the world and hushed it; and I felt
Within the mightiness of the white sun

That smote the land around us and wrought out
A fragrance from the trees, a vital warmth
335 And fullness for the time that was to come,
And a glory for the world beyond the forest.
The present and the future and the past,
Isaac and Archibald, the burning bush,
The Trojans and the walls of Jericho,
340 Were beautifully fused; and all went well
Till Archibald began to fret for Isaac
And said it was a master day for sunstroke.
That was enough to make a mummy smile,
I thought; and I remained hilarious,
345 In face of all precedence and respect,
Till Isaac (who had come to us unheard)
Found he had no tobacco, looked at me
Peculiarly, and asked of Archibald
What ailed the boy to make him chirrup so.
350 From that he told us what a blessed world
The Lord had given us.—"But, Archibald,"
He added, with a sweet severity
That made me think of peach-skins and goose-flesh,
"I'm half afraid you cut those oats of yours
355 A day or two before they were well set."
"They were set well enough," said Archibald,—
And I remarked the process of his nose
Before the words came out. "But never mind
Your neighbor's oats: you stay here in the shade
360 And rest yourself while I go find the cards.
We'll have a little game of seven-up
And let the boy keep count."—"We'll have the game,
Assuredly," said Isaac; "and I think
That I will have a drop of cider, also."

365 They marched away together towards the house
And left me to my childish ruminations

Upon the ways of men. I followed them
Down cellar with my fancy, and then left them
For a fairer vision of all things at once
370 That was anon to be destroyed again
By the sound of voices and of heavy feet—
One of the sounds of life that I remember,
Though I forget so many that rang first
As if they were thrown down to me from Sinai.

375 So I remember, even to this day,
Just how they sounded, how they placed themselves,
And how the game went on while I made marks
And crossed them out, and meanwhile made some
  Trojans.
Likewise I made Ulysses, after Isaac,
380 And a little after Flaxman. Archibald
Was injured when he found himself left out,
But he had no heroics, and I said so:
I told him that his white beard was too long
And too straight down to be like things in Homer.
385 "Quite so," said Isaac.—"Low," said Archibald;
And he threw down a deuce with a deep grin
That showed his yellow teeth and made me happy.
So they played on till a bell rang from the door,
And Archibald said, "Supper."—After that
390 The old men smoked while I sat watching them
And wondered with all comfort what might come
To me, and what might never come to me;
And when the time came for the long walk home
With Isaac in the twilight, I could see
395 The forest and the sunset and the sky-line,
No matter where it was that I was looking:
The flame beyond the boundary, the music,
The foam and the white ships, and two old men
Were things that would not leave me.—And that night

400　There came to me a dream—a shining one,
　　With two old angels in it. They had wings,
　　And they were sitting where a silver light
　　Suffused them, face to face. The wings of one
　　Began to palpitate as I approached,
405　But I was yet unseen when a dry voice
　　Cried thinly, with unpatronizing triumph,
　　"I've got you, Isaac; high, low, jack, and the game."

　　Isaac and Archibald have gone their way
　　To the silence of the loved and well-forgotten.
410　I knew them, and I may have laughed at them;
　　But there's a laughing that has honor in it,
　　And I have no regret for light words now.
　　Rather I think sometimes they may have made
　　Their sport of me;—but they would not do that,
415　They were too old for that. They were old men,
　　And I may laugh at them because I knew them.

AUNT IMOGEN

Aunt Imogen was coming, and therefore
The children—Jane, Sylvester, and Young George—
Were eyes and ears; for there was only one
Aunt Imogen to them in the whole world,
5   And she was in it only for four weeks
In fifty-two. But those great bites of time
Made all September a Queen's Festival;
And they would strive, informally, to make
The most of them.—The mother understood,
10   And wisely stepped away. Aunt Imogen
Was there for only one month in the year,
While she, the mother,—she was always there;
And that was what made all the difference.
She knew it must be so, for Jane had once
15   Expounded it to her so learnedly
That she had looked away from the child's eyes
And thought; and she had thought of many things.

There was a demonstration every time
Aunt Imogen appeared, and there was more
20   Than one this time. And she was at a loss
Just how to name the meaning of it all:
It puzzled her to think that she could be
So much to any crazy thing alive—
Even to her sister's little savages
25   Who knew no better than to be themselves;
But in the midst of her glad wonderment
She found herself besieged and overcome

By two tight arms and one tumultuous head,
And therewith half bewildered and half pained
30 By the joy she felt and by the sudden love
That proved itself in childhood's honest noise.
Jane, by the wings of sex, had reached her first;
And while she strangled her, approvingly,
Sylvester thumped his drum and Young George
howled.
35 But finally, when all was rectified,
And she had stilled the clamor of Young George
By giving him a long ride on her shoulders,
They went together into the old room
That looked across the fields; and Imogen
40 Gazed out with a girl's gladness in her eyes,
Happy to know that she was back once more
Where there were those who knew her, and at last
Had gloriously got away again
From cabs and clattered asphalt for a while;
45 And there she sat and talked and looked and laughed
And made the mother and the children laugh.
Aunt Imogen made everybody laugh.

There was the feminine paradox—that she
Who had so little sunshine for herself
50 Should have so much for others. How it was
That she could make, and feel for making it,
So much of joy for them, and all along
Be covering, like a scar, and while she smiled,
That hungering incompleteness and regret—
55 That passionate ache for something of her own,
For something of herself—she never knew.
She knew that she could seem to make them all
Believe there was no other part of her
Than her persistent happiness; but the why
60 And how she did not know. Still none of them

Could have a thought that she was living down—
Almost as if regret were criminal,
So proud it was and yet so profitless—
The penance of a dream, and that was good.
65 Her sister Jane—the mother of little Jane,
Sylvester, and Young George—might make herself
Believe she knew, for she—well, she was Jane.

Young George, however, did not yield himself
To nourish the false hunger of a ghost
70 That made no good return. He saw too much:
The accumulated wisdom of his years
Had so conclusively made plain to him
The permanent profusion of a world
Where everybody might have everything
75 To do, and almost everything to eat,
That he was jubilantly satisfied
And all unthwarted by adversity.
Young George knew things. The world, he had
        found out
Was a good place, and life was a good game—
80 Particularly when Aunt Imogen
Was in it. And one day it came to pass—
One rainy day when she was holding him
And rocking him—that he, in his own right,
Took it upon himself to tell her so;
85 And something in his way of telling it—
The language, or the tone, or something else—
Gripped like insidious fingers on her throat,
And then went foraging as if to make
A plaything of her heart. Such undeserved
90 And unsophisticated confidence
Went mercilessly home; and had she sat
Before a looking glass, the deeps of it
Could not have shown more clearly to her then

Than one thought-mirrored little glimpse had shown
95 The pang that wrenched her face and filled her eyes
With anguish and intolerable mist.
The blow that she had vaguely thrust aside
Like fright so many times had found her now:
Clean-thrust and final it had come to her
100 From a child's lips at last, as it had come
Never before, and as it might be felt
Never again. Some grief, like some delight,
Stings hard but once: to custom after that
The rapture or the pain submits itself,
105 And we are wiser than we were before.
And Imogen was wiser; though at first
Her dream-defeating wisdom was indeed
A thankless heritage: there was no sweet,
No bitter now; nor was there anything
110 To make a daily meaning for her life—
Till truth, like Harlequin, leapt out somehow
From ambush and threw sudden savor to it—
But the blank taste of time. There were no dreams,
No phantoms in her future any more:
115 One clinching revelation of what was
One by-flash of irrevocable chance,
Had acridly but honestly foretold
The mystical fulfilment of a life
That might have once . . . But that was all gone by:
120 There was no need of reaching back for that:
The triumph was not hers: there was no love
Save borrowed love: there was no might have been.

But there was yet Young George—and he had gone
Conveniently to sleep, like a good boy;
125 And there was yet Sylvester with his drum,
And there was frowzle-headed little Jane;
And there was Jane the sister, and the mother,—

Her sister, and the mother of them all.
They were not hers, not even one of them:
130   She was not born to be so much as that,
For she was born to be Aunt Imogen.
Now she could see the truth and look at it;
Now she could make stars out where once had palled
A future's emptiness; now she could share
135   With others—ah, the others!—to the end
The largess of a woman who could smile;
Now it was hers to dance the folly down,
And all the murmuring; now it was hers
To be Aunt Imogen.—So, when Young George
140   Woke up and blinked at her with his big eyes,
And smiled to see the way she blinked at him,
'T was only in old concord with the stars
That she took hold of him and held him close,
Close to herself, and crushed him till he laughed.

THE GROWTH OF "LORRAINE"

I

While I stood listening, discreetly dumb,
Lorraine was having the last word with me:
"I know," she said, "I know it, but you see
Some creatures are born fortunate, and some
Are born to be found out and overcome,—
Born to be slaves, to let the rest go free;
And if I'm one of them (and I must be)
You may as well forget me and go home.

"You tell me not to say these things, I know,
But I should never try to be content:
I've gone too far; the life would be too slow.
Some could have done it—some girls have the stuff;
But I can't do it: I don't know enough.
I'm going to the devil."—And she went.

II

I did not half believe her when she said
That I should never hear from her again;
Nor when I found a letter from Lorraine,
Was I surprised or grieved at what I read:
"Dear friend, when you find this, I shall be dead.
You are too far away to make me stop.
They say that one drop—think of it, one drop!—
Will be enough,—but I'll take five instead.

44

"You do not frown because I call you friend,
For I would have you glad that I still keep
25   Your memory, and even at the end—
Impenitent, sick, shattered—cannot curse
The love that flings, for better or for worse,
This worn-out, cast-out flesh of mine to sleep."

ERASMUS

When he protested, not too solemnly,
That for a world's achieving maintenance
The crust of overdone divinity
Lacked aliment, they called it recreance;
5 And when he chose through his own glass to scan
Sick Europe, and reduced, unyieldingly,
The monk within the cassock to the man
Within the monk, they called it heresy.

And when he made so perilously bold
10 As to be scattered forth in black and white,
Good fathers looked askance at him and rolled
Their inward eyes in anguish and affright;
There were some of them did shake at what was told
And they shook best who knew that he was right.

THE WOMAN AND THE WIFE

I—THE EXPLANATION

"You thought we knew," she said, "but we were
    wrong.
This we can say, the rest we do not say;
Nor do I let you throw yourself away
Because you love me. Let us both be strong,
5   And we shall find in sorrow, before long,
Only the price Love ruled that we should pay:
The dark is at the end of every day,
And silence is the end of every song.

"You ask me for one proof that I speak right,
10   But I can answer only what I know;
You look for just one lie to make black white,
But I can tell you only what is true—
God never made me for the wife of you.
This we can say,—believe me! . . . Tell me so!"

II—THE ANNIVERSARY

15   "Give me the truth, whatever it may be.
You thought we knew, now tell me what you miss:
You are the one to tell me what it is—
You are a man, and you have married me.
What is it worth to-night that you can see
20   More marriage in the dream of one dead kiss

Than in a thousand years of life like this?
Passion has turned the lock, Pride keeps the key.

"Whatever I have said or left unsaid,
Whatever I have done or left undone,—
25   Tell me. Tell me the truth. . . . Are you afraid?
Do you think that Love was ever fed with lies
But hunger lived thereafter in his eyes?
Do you ask me to take moonlight for the sun?"

MERLIN

(Conclusion)

He stared away into the west again,
Where now no crimson cloud or phantom town
Deceived his eyes. Above a living town
There were gray clouds and ultimate suspense,
5   And a cold wind was coming. Dagonet,
Now crouched at Merlin's feet in his dejection,
Saw multiplying lights far down below,
Where lay the fevered streets. At length he felt
On his lean shoulder Merlin's tragic hand
10   And trembled, knowing that a few more days
Would see the last of Arthur and the first
Of Modred, whose dark patience had attained
To one precarious half of what he sought:
"And even the Queen herself may fall to him,"
15   Dagonet murmured.—"The Queen fall to Modred?
Is that your only fear tonight?" said Merlin;
"She may, but not for long."—"No, not my fear;
For I fear nothing. But I wish no fate
Like that for any woman the King loves,
20   Although she be the scourge and the end of him
That you saw coming, as I see it now."
Dagonet shook, but he would have no tears,
He swore, for any king, queen, knave, or wizard—
Albeit he was a stranger among those
25   Who laughed at him because he was a fool.
"You said the truth, I cannot leave you now,"
He stammered, and was angry for the tears
That mocked his will and choked him.

                                        Merlin smiled,
30 Faintly, and for the moment: "Dagonet,
    I need your word as one of Arthur's knights
    That you will go on with me to the end
    Of my short way, and say unto no man
    Or woman that you found or saw me here.
35 No good would follow, for a doubt would live
    Unstifled of my loyalty to him
    Whose deeds are wrought for those who are to come;
    And many who see not what I have seen,
    Or what you see tonight, would prattle on
40 For ever, and their children after them,
    Of what might once have been had I gone down
    With you to Camelot to see the King.
    I came to see the King,—but why see kings?
    All this that was to be is what I saw
45 Before there was an Arthur to be king,
    And so to be a mirror wherein men
    May see themselves, and pause. If they see not,
    Or if they do see and they ponder not,—
    I saw; but I was neither Fate nor God.
50 I saw too much; and this would be the end,
    Were there to be an end. I saw myself—
    A sight no other man has ever seen;
    And through the dark that lay beyond myself
    I saw two fires that are to light the world."

55 On Dagonet the silent hand of Merlin
    Weighed now as living iron that held him down
    With a primeval power. Doubt, wonderment,
    Impatience, and a self-accusing sorrow
    Born of an ancient love, possessed and held him
60 Until his love was more than he could name,
    And he was Merlin's fool, not Arthur's now:
    "Say what you will, I say that I'm the fool

Of Merlin, King of Nowhere; which is Here.
With you for king and me for court, what else
65 Have we to sigh for but a place to sleep?
I know a tarvern that will take us in;
And on the morrow I shall follow you
Until I die for you. And when I die . . ."—
"Well, Dagonet, the King is listening."—
70 And Dagonet answered, hearing in the words
Of Merlin a grave humor and a sound
Of graver pity, "I shall die a fool."
He heard what might have been a father's laugh,
Faintly behind him; and the living weight
75 Of Merlin's hand was lifted. They arose,
And, saying nothing, found a groping way
Down through the gloom together. Fiercer now,
The wind was like a flying animal
That beat the two of them incessantly
80 With icy wings, and bit them as they went.
The rock above them was an empty place
Where neither seer nor fool should view again
The stricken city. Colder blew the wind
Across the world, and on it heavier lay
85 The shadow and the burden of the night;
And there was darkness over Camelot.

THE MASTER

(Lincoln)

A flying word from here and there
Had sown the name at which we sneered,
But soon the name was everywhere,
To be reviled and then revered:
5   A presence to be loved and feared,
We cannot hide it, or deny
That we, the gentlemen who jeered,
May be forgotten by and by.

He came when days were perilous
10   And hearts of men were sore beguiled;
And having made his note of us,
He pondered and was reconciled.
Was ever master yet so mild
As he, and so untamable?
15   We doubted, even when he smiled,
Not knowing what he knew so well.

He knew that undeceiving fate
Would shame us whom he served unsought;
He knew that he must wince and wait—
20   The jest of those for whom he fought;
He knew devoutly what he thought
Of us and of our ridicule;
He knew that we must all be taught
Like little children in a school.

25 We gave a glamour to the task
That he encountered and saw through,
But little of us did he ask,
And little did we ever do.
And what appears if we review
30 The season when we railed and chaffed?
It is the face of one who knew
That we were learning while we laughed.

The face that in our vision feels
Again the venom that we flung,
35 Transfigured to the world reveals
The vigilance to which we clung.
Shrewd, hallowed, harassed, and among
The mysteries that are untold,
The face we see was never young
40 Nor could it wholly have been old.

For he, to whom we had applied
Our shopman's test of age and worth,
Was elemental when he died,
As he was ancient at his birth:
45 The saddest among kings of earth,
Bowed with a galling crown, this man
Met rancor with a cryptic mirth,
Laconic—and Olympian.

The love, the grandeur, and the fame
50 Are bounded by the world alone;
The calm, the smouldering, and the flame
Of awful patience were his own:
With him they are forever flown
Past all our fond self-shadowings,
55 Wherewith we cumber the Unknown
As with inept, Icarian wings.

For we were not as other men:
'Twas ours to soar and his to see;
But we are coming down again,
60   And we shall come down pleasantly;
Nor shall we longer disagree
On what it is to be sublime,
But flourish in our perigee
And have one Titan at a time.

Supposed to have been written not long after the Civil War. [Robinson's note.]

CALVERLY'S

We go no more to Calverly's,
For there the lights are few and low;
And who are there to see by them,
Or what they see, we do not know.
5   Poor strangers of another tongue
May now creep in from anywhere,
And we, forgotten, be no more
Than twilight on a ruin there.

We two, the remnant. All the rest
10   Are cold and quiet. You nor I,
Nor fiddle now, nor flagon-lid,
May ring them back from where they lie.
No fame delays oblivion
For them, but something yet survives:
15   A record written fair, could we
But read the book of scattered lives.

There'll be a page for Leffingwell,
And one for Lingard, the Moon-calf;
And who knows what for Clavering,
20   Who died because he couldn't laugh?
Who knows or cares? No sign is here,
No face, no voice, no memory;
No Lingard with his eerie joy,
No Clavering, no Calverly.

25 We cannot have them here with us
   To say where their light lives are gone,
   Or if they be of other stuff
   Than are the moons of Ilion.
   So, be their place of one estate
30 With ashes, echoes, and old wars,—
   Or ever we be of the night,
   Or we be lost among the stars.

UNCLE ANANIAS

His words were magic and his heart was true,
   And everywhere he wandered he was blessed.
Out of all ancient men my childhood knew
   I choose him and I mark him for the best.
₅ Of all authoritative liars, too,
   I crown him loveliest.

How fondly I remember the delight
   That always glorified him in the spring;
The joyous courage and the benedight
₁₀   Profusion of his faith in everything!
He was a good old man, and it was right
   That he should have his fling.

And often, underneath the apple-trees,
   When we surprised him in the summer time,
₁₅ With what superb magnificence and ease
   He sinned enough to make the day sublime!
And if he liked us there about his knees,
   Truly it was no crime.

All summer long we loved him for the same
₂₀   Perennial inspiration of his lies;
And when the russet wealth of autumn came,
   There flew but fairer visions to our eyes—
Multiple, tropical, winged with a feathery flame,
   Like birds of paradise.

25 So to the sheltered end of many a year
        He charmed the seasons out with pageantry
    Wearing upon his forehead, with no fear,
        The laurel of approved iniquity.
    And every child who knew him, far or near,
30   Did love him faithfully.

THE WHIP

The doubt you fought so long
The cynic net you cast,
The tyranny, the wrong,
The ruin, they are past;
5   And here you are at last,
Your blood no longer vexed.
The coffin has you fast,
The clod will have you next.

But fear you not the clod,
10   Nor ever doubt the grave:
The roses and the sod
Will not forswear the wave.
The gift the river gave
Is now but theirs to cover:
15   The mistress and the slave
Are gone now, and the lover.

You left the two to find
Their own way to the brink
Then—shall I call you blind?—
20   You chose to plunge and sink.
God knows the gall we drink
Is not the mead we cry for,
Nor was it, I should think—
For you—a thing to die for.

25   Could we have done the same,
        Had we been in your place?—
        This funeral of your name
        Throws no light on the case.
        Could we have made the chase,
30   And felt then as you felt?—
        But what's this on your face,
        Blue, curious, like a welt?

        There were some ropes of sand
        Recorded long ago,
35   But none, I understand,
        Of water. Is it so?
        And she—she struck the blow,
        You but a neck behind . . .
        You saw the river flow—
40   Still, shall I call you blind?

THE WHITE LIGHTS

(Broadway, 1906)

When in from Delos came the gold
That held the dream of Pericles,
When first Athenian ears were told
The tumult of Euripides,
5   When men met Aristophanes,
Who fledged them with immortal quills—
Here, where the time knew none of these,
There were some islands and some hills.

When Rome went ravening to see
10   The sons of mothers end their days,
When Flaccus bade Leuconoë
To banish her Chaldean ways,
When first the pearled, alembic phrase
Of Maro into music ran—
15   Here there was neither blame nor praise
For Rome, or for the Mantuan.

When Avon, like a faery floor,
Lay freighted, for the eyes of One,
With galleons laden long before
20   By moonlit wharves in Avalon—
Here, where the white lights have begun
To seethe a way for something fair,
No prophet knew, from what was done,
That there was triumph in the air.

EXIT

For what we owe to other days,
Before we poisoned him with praise,
May we who shrank to find him weak
Remember that he cannot speak.

5   For envy that we may recall,
And for our faith before the fall,
May we who are alive be slow
To tell what we shall never know.

For penance he would not confess,
10   And for the fateful emptiness
Of early triumph undermined,
May we now venture to be kind.

LEONORA

They have made for Leonora this low dwelling in the
    ground,
And with cedar they have woven the four walls
    round.
Like a little dryad hiding she'll be wrapped all in
    green,
Better kept and longer valued than by ways that
    would have been.

5   They will come with many roses in the early
    afternoon,
They will come with pinks and lilies and with
    Leonora soon;
And as long as beauty's garments over beauty's limbs
    are thrown,
There'll be lilies that are liars, and the rose will have
    its own.

There will be a wondrous quiet in the house that they
    have made,
10   And to-night will be a darkness in the place where
    she'll be laid;
But the builders, looking forward into time, could
    only see
Darker nights for Leonora than to-night shall ever be.

DOCTOR OF BILLIARDS

Of all among the fallen from on high,
We count you last and leave you to regain
Your born dominion of a life made vain
By three spheres of insidious ivory.
5 You dwindle to the lesser tragedy—
Content, you say. We call, but you remain.
Nothing alive gone wrong could be so plain,
Or quite so blasted with absurdity.

You click away the kingdom that is yours,
10 And you click off your crown for cap and bells;
You smile, who are still master of the feast,
And for your smile we credit you the least;
But when your false, unhallowed laugh occurs,
We seem to think there may be something else.

HOW ANNANDALE WENT OUT

"They called it Annandale—and I was there
To flourish, to find words, and to attend:
Liar, physician, hypocrite, and friend,
I watched him; and the sight was not so fair
As one or two that I have seen elsewhere:
An apparatus not for me to mend—
A wreck, with hell between him and the end,
Remained of Annandale; and I was there.

"I knew the ruin as I knew the man;
So put the two together, if you can,
Remembering the worst you know of me.
Now view yourself as I was, on the spot—
With a slight kind of engine. Do you see?
Like this . . . You wouldn't hang me? I thought not."

ALMA MATER

He knocked, and I beheld him at the door—
A vision for the gods to verify.
"What battered ancientry is this," thought I,
"And when, if ever, did we meet before?"
But ask him as I might, I got no more
For answer than a moaning and a cry:
Too late to parley, but in time to die,
He staggered, and lay shapeless on the floor.

When had I known him? And what brought him
    here?
Love, warning, malediction, hunger, fear?
Surely I never thwarted such as he?—
Again, what soiled obscurity was this:
Out of what scum, and up from what abyss,
Had they arrived—these rags of memory?

MINIVER CHEEVY

Miniver Cheevy, child of scorn,
  Grew lean while he assailed the seasons;
He wept that he was ever born,
  And he had reasons.

5 Miniver loved the days of old
  When swords were bright and steeds were prancing;
The vision of a warrior bold
  Would set him dancing.

Miniver sighed for what was not,
10 And dreamed, and rested from his labors;
He dreamed of Thebes and Camelot,
  And Priam's neighbors.

Miniver mourned the ripe renown
  That made so many a name so fragrant;
15 He mourned Romance, now on the town,
  And Art, a vagrant.

Miniver loved the Medici,
  Albeit he had never seen one;
He would have sinned incessantly
20 Could he have been one.

Miniver cursed the commonplace
  And eyed a khaki suit with loathing;
He missed the mediaeval grace
  Of iron clothing.

25 Miniver scorned the gold he sought,
        But sore annoyed was he without it;
    Miniver thought, and thought, and thought,
        And thought about it.

    Miniver Cheevy, born too late,
30   Scratched his head and kept on thinking;
    Miniver coughed, and called it fate,
        And kept on drinking.

THE PILOT

From the Past and Unavailing
Out of cloudland we are steering:
After groping, after fearing,
Into starlight we come trailing,
5   And we find the stars are true.
Still, O comrade, what of you?
You are gone, but we are sailing,
And the old ways are all new.

For the Lost and Unreturning
10   We have drifted, we have waited;
Uncommanded and unrated,
We have tossed and wandered, yearning
For a charm that comes no more
From the old lights by the shore:
15   We have shamed ourselves in learning
What you knew so long before.

For the Breed of the Far-going
Who are strangers, and all brothers,
May forget no more than others
20   Who looked seaward with eyes flowing.
But are brothers to bewail
One who fought so foul a gale?
You have won beyond our knowing,
You are gone, but yet we sail.

VICKERY'S MOUNTAIN

Blue in the west the mountain stands,
  And through the long twilight
Vickery sits with folded hands,
  And Vickery's eyes are bright.

5 Bright, for he knows what no man else
    On earth as yet may know:
There's a golden word that he never tells,
  And a gift that he will not show.

He dreams of honor and wealth and fame,
10   He smiles, and well he may;
For to Vickery once a sick man came
  Who did not go away.

The day before the day to be,
  "Vickery," said the guest,
15 "You know as you live what's left of me—
  And you shall know the rest.

"You know as you live that I have come
  To this we call the end.
No doubt you have found me troublesome,
20   But you've also found a friend;

"For we shall give and you shall take
  The gold that is in view;

The mountain there and I shall make
A golden man of you.

25 "And you shall leave a friend behind
Who neither frets nor feels;
And you shall move among your kind
With hundreds at your heels.

"Now this that I have written here
30 Tells all that need be told;
So, Vickery, take the way that's clear.
And be a man of gold."

Vickery turned his eyes again
To the far mountain-side,
35 And wept a tear for worthy men
Defeated and defied.

Since then a crafty score of years
Have come, and they have gone;
But Vickery counts no lost arrears:
40 He lingers and lives on.

Blue in the west the mountain stands,
Familiar as a face.
Blue, but Vickery knows what sands
Are golden at its base.

45 He dreams and lives upon the day
When he shall walk with kings.
Vickery smiles—and well he may.
The life-caged linnet sings.

Vickery thinks the time will come
50 To go for what is his;

But hovering, unseen hands at home
  Will hold him where he is.

There's a golden word that he never tells
  And a gift that he will not show.
55   All to be given to some one else—
  And Vickery not to know.

FOR A DEAD LADY

No more with overflowing light
Shall fill the eyes that now are faded,
Nor shall another's fringe with night
Their woman-hidden world as they did.
5   No more shall quiver down the days
The flowing wonder of her ways,
Whereof no language may requite
The shifting and the many-shaded.

The grace, divine, definitive,
10   Clings only as a faint forestalling;
The laugh that love could not forgive
Is hushed, and answers to no calling;
The forehead and the little ears
Have gone where Saturn keeps the years;
15   The breast where roses could not live
Has done with rising and with falling.

The beauty, shattered by the laws
That have creation in their keeping,
No longer trembles at applause,
20   Or over children that are sleeping;
And we who delve in beauty's lore
Know all that we have known before
Of what inexorable cause
Makes Time so vicious in his reaping.

TWO GARDENS IN LINNDALE

Two brothers, Oakes and Oliver,
Two gentle men as ever were,
Would roam no longer, but abide
In Linndale, where their fathers died,
5   And each would be a gardener.

"Now first we fence the garden through,
With this for me and that for you,"
Said Oliver.—"Divine!" said Oakes,
"And I, while I raise artichokes,
10   Will do what I was born to do."

"But this is not the soil, you know,"
Said Oliver, "to make them grow:
The parent of us, who is dead,
Compassionately shook his head
15   Once on a time and told me so."

"I hear you, gentle Oliver,"
Said Oakes, "and in your character
I find as fair a thing indeed
As ever bloomed and ran to seed
20   Since Adam was a gardener.

"Still, whatsoever I find there,
Forgive me if I do not share
The knowing gloom that you take on
Of one who doubted and is done:
25   For chemistry meets every prayer."

"Sometimes a rock will meet a plough,"
Said Oliver; "but anyhow
'Tis here we are, 'tis here we live,
With each to take and each to give:
30   There's no room for a quarrel now.

"I leave you in all gentleness
To science and a ripe success.
Now God be with you, brother Oakes,
With you and with your artichokes:
35   You have the vision, more or less."

"By fate, that gives to me no choice,
I have the vision and the voice:
Dear Oliver, believe in me,
And we shall see what we shall see;
40   Henceforward let us both rejoice."

"But first, while we have joy to spare
We'll plant a little here and there;
And if you be not in the wrong,
We'll sing together such a song
45   As no man yet sings anywhere."

They planted and with fruitful eyes
Attended each his enterprise.
"Now days will come and days will go,
And many a way be found, we know,"
50   Said Oakes, "and we shall sing, likewise."

"The days will go, the years will go,
And many a song be sung, we know,"
Said Oliver; "and if there be
Good harvesting for you and me,
55   Who cares if we sing loud or low?"

They planted once, and twice, and thrice,
Like amateurs in paradise;
And every spring, fond, foiled, elate,
Said Oakes, "We are in tune with Fate:
60   One season longer will suffice."

Year after year 'twas all the same:
With none to envy, none to blame,
They lived along in innocence,
Nor ever once forgot the fence,
65   Till on a day the Stranger came.

He came to greet them where they were,
And he too was a Gardener:
He stood between these gentle men,
He stayed a little while, and then
70   The land was all for Oliver.

'Tis Oliver who tills alone
Two gardens that are now his own;
'Tis Oliver who sows and reaps
And listens, while the other sleeps,
75   For songs undreamed of and unknown.

'Tis he, the gentle anchorite,
Who listens for them day and night;
But most he hears them in the dawn,
When from his trees across the lawn
80   Birds ring the chorus of the light.

He cannot sing without the voice,
But he may worship and rejoice
For patience in him to remain,
The chosen heir of age and pain,
85   Instead of Oakes—who had no choice.

'Tis Oliver who sits beside
The other's grave at eventide,
And smokes, and wonders what new race
Will have two gardens, by God's grace,
90   In Linndale, where their fathers died.

And often, while he sits and smokes,
He sees the ghost of gentle Oakes
Uprooting, with a restless hand,
Soft, shadowy flowers in a land
95   Of asphodels and artichokes.

FLAMMONDE

The man Flammonde, from God knows where,
With firm address and foreign air,
With news of nations in his talk
And something royal in his walk,
5   With glint of iron in his eyes,
But never doubt, nor yet surprise,
Appeared, and stayed, and held his head
As one by kings accredited.

Erect, with his alert repose
10   About him, and about his clothes,
He pictured all tradition hears
Of what we owe to fifty years.
His cleansing heritage of taste
Paraded neither want nor waste;
15   And what he needed for his fee
To live, he borrowed graciously.

He never told us what he was,
Or what mischance, or other cause,
Had banished him from better days
20   To play the Prince of Castaways.
Meanwhile he played surpassing well
A part, for most, unplayable;
In fine, one pauses, half afraid
To say for certain that he played.

25 For that, one may as well forgo
    Conviction as to yes or no;
    Nor can I say just how intense
    Would then have been the difference
    To several, who, having striven
30 In vain to get what he was given,
    Would see the stranger taken on
    By friends not easy to be won.

    Moreover, many a malcontent
    He soothed and found munificent;
35 His courtesy beguiled and foiled
    Suspicion that his years were soiled;
    His mien distinguished any crowd,
    His credit strengthened when he bowed;
    And women, young and old, were fond
40 Of looking at the man Flammonde.

    There was a woman in our town
    On whom the fashion was to frown;
    But while our talk renewed the tinge
    Of a long-faded scarlet fringe,
45 The man Flammonde saw none of that,
    And what he saw we wondered at—
    That none of us, in her distress,
    Could hide or find our littleness.

    There was a boy that all agreed
50 Had shut within him the rare seed
    Of learning. We could understand,
    But none of us could lift a hand.
    The man Flammonde appraised the youth,
    And told a few of us the truth;
55 And thereby, for a little gold,
    A flowered future was unrolled.

There were two citizens who fought
For years and years, and over nought;
They made life awkward for their friends,
And shortened their own dividends.
The man Flammonde said what was wrong
Should be made right; nor was it long
Before they were again in line,
And had each other in to dine.

And these I mention are but four
Of many out of many more.
So much for them. But what of him—
So firm in every look and limb?
What small satanic sort of kink
Was in his brain? What broken link
Withheld him from the destinies
That came so near to being his?

What was he, when we came to sift
His meaning, and to note the drift
Of incommunicable ways
That make us ponder while we praise?
Why was it that his charm revealed
Somehow the surface of a shield?
What was it that we never caught?
What was he, and what was he not?

How much it was of him we met
We cannot ever know; nor yet
Shall all he gave us quite atone
For what was his, and his alone;
Nor need we now, since he knew best,
Nourish an ethical unrest:
Rarely at once will nature give
The power to be Flammonde and live.

We cannot know how much we learn
90   From those who never will return,
Until a flash of unforeseen
Remembrance falls on what has been.
We've each a darkening hill to climb;
And this is why, from time to time
95   In Tilbury Town, we look beyond
Horizons for the man Flammonde.

THE GIFT OF GOD

Blessed with a joy that only she
Of all alive shall ever know,
She wears a proud humility
For what it was that willed it so,—
5   That her degree should be so great
Among the favored of the Lord
That she may scarcely bear the weight
Of her bewildering reward.

As one apart, immune, alone,
10   Or featured for the shining ones,
And like to none that she has known
Of other women's other sons,—
The firm fruition of her need
He shines anointed; and he blurs
15   Her vision, till it seems indeed
A sacrilege to call him hers.

She fears a little for so much
Of what is best, and hardly dares
To think of him as one to touch
20   With aches, indignities, and cares;
She sees him rather at the goal,
Still shining; and her dream foretells
The proper shining of a soul
Where nothing ordinary dwells.

25 Perchance a canvass of the town
    Would find him far from flags and shouts,
    And leave him only the renown
    Of many smiles and many doubts;
    Perchance the crude and common tongue
30 Would havoc strangely with his worth;
    But she, with innocence unwrung,
    Would read his name around the earth.

    And others, knowing how this youth
    Would shine, if love could make him great,
35 When caught and tortured for the truth
    Would only writhe and hesitate;
    While she, arranging for his days
    What centuries could not fulfill,
    Transmutes him with her faith and praise,
40 And has him shining where she will.

    She crowns him with her gratefulness,
    And says again that life is good;
    And should the gift of God be less
    In him than in her motherhood,
45 His fame, though vague, will not be small,
    As upward through her dream he fares,
    Half clouded with a crimson fall
    Of roses thrown on marble stairs.

JOHN GORHAM

"Tell me what you're doing over here, John Gorham,
Sighing hard and seeming to be sorry when you're
     not;
Make me laugh or let me go now, for long faces in the
     moonlight
Are a sign for me to say again a word that you
     forgot."—

5   "I'm over here to tell you what the moon already
May have said or maybe shouted ever since a year ago;
I'm over here to tell you what you are, Jane Wayland,
And to make you rather sorry, I should say, for
     being so."—

"Tell me what you're saying to me now, John
     Gorham,
10 Or you'll never see as much of me as ribbons any
     more;
I'll vanish in as many ways as I have toes and fingers,
And you'll not follow far for one where flocks have
     been before."—

"I'm sorry now you never saw the flocks, Jane
     Wayland,
But you're the one to make of them as many as you
     need.
15 And then about the vanishing. It's I who mean to
     vanish;

And when I'm here no longer you'll be done with me
    indeed."—

"That's a way to tell me what I am, John Gorham!
How am I to know myself until I make you smile?
Try to look as if the moon were making faces at you,
20   And a little more as if you meant to stay a little
    while."—

"You are what it is that over rose-blown gardens
Makes a pretty flutter for a season in the sun;
You are what it is that with a mouse, Jane Wayland,
Catches him and lets him go and eats him up
    for fun."—

25   "Sure I never took you for a mouse, John Gorham;
All you say is easy, but so far from being true
That I wish you wouldn't ever be again the one to
    think so;
For it isn't cats and butterflies that I would be
    to you."—

"All your little animals are in one picture—
30   One I've had before me since a year ago to-night;
And the picture where they live will be of you, Jane
    Wayland,
Till you find a way to kill them or to keep them out
    of sight."—

"Won't you ever see me as I am, John Gorham,
Leaving out the foolishness and all I never meant?
35   Somewhere in me there's a woman, if you know the
    way to find her.
Will you like me any better if I prove it and
    repent?"—

"I doubt if I shall ever have the time, Jane Wayland;
And I dare say all this moonlight lying round us
    might as well
Fall for nothing on the shards of broken urns that are
    forgotten,
40   As on two that have no longer much of anything to
    tell."

STAFFORD'S CABIN

Once there was a cabin here, and once there was
    a man;
And something happened here before my memory
    began.
Time has made the two of them the fuel of one flame
And all we have of them is now a legend and a name.

5   All I have to say is what an old man said to me,
And that would seem to be as much as there will
    ever be.
"Fifty years ago it was we found it where it sat."—
And forty years ago it was old Archibald said that

"An apple tree that's yet alive saw something, I
    suppose,
10   Of what it was that happened there, and what no
    mortal knows
Some one on the mountain heard far off a master
    shriek,
And then there was a light that showed the way for
    men to seek.

"We found it in the morning with an iron bar behind,
And there were chains around it; but no search could
    ever find,
15   Either in the ashes that were left, or anywhere,
A sign to tell of who or what had been with Stafford
    there.

"Stafford was a likely man with ideas of his own—
Though I could never like the kind that likes to live
    alone;
And when you met, you found his eyes were always
    on your shoes,
As if they did the talking when he asked you for the
    news.

"That's all, my son. Were I to talk for half a hundred
    years
I'd never clear away from there the cloud that never
    clears.
We buried what was left of it,—the bar, too, and the
    chains;
And only for the apple tree there's nothing that
    remains."

Forty years ago it was I heard the old man say,
"That's all, my son."—And here again I find the place
    to-day,
Deserted and told only by the tree that knows the
    most,
And overgrown with golden-rod as if there were no
    ghost.

HILLCREST

(To Mrs. Edward MacDowell)

No sound of any storm that shakes
Old island walls with older seas
Comes here where now September makes
An island in a sea of trees.

5   Between the sunlight and the shade
A man may learn till he forgets
The roaring of a world remade,
And all his ruins and regrets;

And if he still remembers here
10   Poor fights he may have won or lost,—
If he be ridden with the fear
Of what some other fight may cost,—

If, eager to confuse too soon,
What he has known with what may be,
15   He reads a planet out of tune
For cause of his jarred harmony,—

If here he venture to unroll
His index of adagios,
And he be given to console
20   Humanity with what he knows,—

He may by contemplation learn
A little more than what he knew,
And even see great oaks return
To acorns out of which they grew.

²⁵ He may, if he but listen well,
Through twilight and the silence here,
Be told what there are none may tell
To vanity's impatient ear;

And he may never dare again
³⁰ Say what awaits him, or be sure
What sunlit labyrinth of pain
He may not enter and endure.

Who knows to-day from yesterday
May learn to count no thing too strange:
³⁵ Love builds of what Time takes away,
Till Death itself is less than Change.

Who sees enough in his duress
May go as far as dreams have gone;
Who sees a little may do less
⁴⁰ Than many who are blind have done;

Who sees unchastened here the soul
Triumphant has no other sight
Than has a child who sees the whole
World radiant with his own delight.

⁴⁵ Far journeys and hard wandering
Await him in whose crude surmise
Peace, like a mask, hides everything
That is and has been from his eyes;

And all his wisdom is unfound,
⁵⁰ Or like a web that error weaves
On airy looms that have a sound
No louder now than falling leaves.

EROS TURANNOS

She fears him, and will always ask
    What fated her to choose him;
She meets in his engaging mask
    All reasons to refuse him;
5 But what she meets and what she fears
Are less than are the downward years,
Drawn slowly to the foamless weirs
    Of age, were she to lose him.

Between a blurred sagacity
10   That once had power to sound him,
And Love, that will not let him be
    The Judas that she found him,
Her pride assuages her almost,
As if it were alone the cost.—
15 He sees that he will not be lost,
    And waits and looks around him.

A sense of ocean and old trees
    Envelops and allures him;
Tradition, touching all he sees,
20   Beguiles and reassures him;
And all her doubts of what he says
Are dimmed with what she knows of days—
Till even prejudice delays
    And fades, and she secures him.

The falling leaf inaugurates
        The reign of her confusion;
    The pounding wave reverberates
        The dirge of her illusion;
    And home, where passion lived and died,
30   Becomes a place where she can hide,
    While all the town and harbor side
        Vibrate with her seclusion.

    We tell you, tapping on our brows,
        The story as it should be,—
35   As if the story of a house
        Were told, or ever could be;
    We'll have no kindly veil between
    Her visions and those we have seen,—
    As if we guessed what hers have been,
40   Or what they are or would be.

    Meanwhile we do no harm; for they
        That with a god have striven,
    Not hearing much of what we say,
        Take what the god has given;
45   Though like waves breaking it may be,
    Or like a changed familiar tree,
    Or like a stairway to the sea
        Where down the blind are driven.

THE UNFORGIVEN

When he, who is the unforgiven,
Beheld her first, he found her fair:
No promise ever dreamt in heaven
Could then have lured him anywhere
5   That would have been away from there;
And all his wits had lightly striven,
Foiled with her voice, and eyes, and hair.

There's nothing in the saints and sages
To meet the shafts her glances had,
10   Or such as hers have had for ages
To blind a man till he be glad,
And humble him till he be mad.
The story would have many pages,
And would be neither good nor bad.

15   And, having followed, you would find him
Where properly the play begins;
But look for no red light behind him—
No fumes of many-colored sins,
Fanned high by screaming violins.
20   God knows what good it was to blind him,
Or whether man or woman wins.

And by the same eternal token,
Who knows just how it will all end?—
This drama of hard words unspoken,
25   This fireside farce, without a friend

Or enemy to comprehend
What augurs when two lives are broken,
And fear finds nothing left to mend.

He stares in vain for what awaits him,
30 And sees in Love a coin to toss;
He smiles, and her cold hush berates him
Beneath his hard half of the cross;
They wonder why it ever was;
And she, the unforgiving, hates him
35 More for her lack than for her loss.

He feeds with pride his indecision,
And shrinks from what will not occur,
Bequeathing with infirm derision
His ashes to the days that were,
40 Before she made him prisoner;
And labors to retrieve the vision
That he must once have had of her.

He waits, and there awaits an ending,
And he knows neither what nor when;
45 But no magicians are attending
To make him see as he saw then,
And he will never find again
The face that once had been the rending
Of all his purpose among men.

50 He blames her not, nor does he chide her,
And she has nothing new to say;
If he were Bluebeard he could hide her,
But that's not written in the play,
And there will be no change to-day;
55 Although, to the serene outsider,
There still would seem to be a way.

VETERAN SIRENS

The ghost of Ninon would be sorry now
To laugh at them, were she to see them here,
So brave and so alert for learning how
To fence with reason for another year.

5   Age offers a far comelier diadem
Than theirs; but anguish has no eye for grace,
When time's malicious mercy cautions them
To think a while of number and of space.

The burning hope, the worn expectancy,
10   The martyred humor, and the maimed allure,
Cry out for time to end his levity,
And age to soften its investiture;

But they, though others fade and are still fair,
Defy their fairness and are unsubdued;
15   Although they suffer, they may not forswear
The patient ardor of the unpursued.

Poor flesh, to fight the calendar so long;
Poor vanity, so quaint and yet so brave;
Poor folly, so deceived and yet so strong,
20   So far from Ninon and so near the grave.

ANOTHER DARK LADY

Think not, because I wonder where you fled,
That I would lift a pin to see you there;
You may, for me, be prowling anywhere,
So long as you show not your little head:
5   No dark and evil story of the dead
Would leave you less pernicious or less fair—
Not even Lilith, with her famous hair;
And Lilith was the devil, I have read.

I cannot hate you, for I loved you then.
10   The woods were golden then. There was a road
Through beeches; and I said their smooth feet showed
Like yours. Truth must have heard me from afar,
For I shall never have to learn again
That yours are cloven as no beech's are.

THE DARK HOUSE

Where a faint light shines alone,
Dwells a Demon I have known.
Most of you had better say
"The Dark House," and go your way.
5   Do not wonder if I stay.

For I know the Demon's eyes,
And their lure that never dies.
Banish all your fond alarms,
For I know the foiling charms
10   Of her eyes and of her arms,

And I know that in one room
Burns a lamp as in a tomb;
And I see the shadow glide,
Back and forth, of one denied
15   Power to find himself outside.

There he is who is my friend,
Damned, he fancies, to the end—
Vanquished, ever since a door
Closed, he thought, for evermore
20   On the life that was before.

And the friend who knows him best
Sees him as he sees the rest
Who are striving to be wise
While a Demon's arms and eyes
25   Hold them as a web would flies.

All the words of all the world,
Aimed together and then hurled,
Would be stiller in his ears
Than a closing of still shears
30   On a thread made out of years.

But there lives another sound,
More compelling, more profound;
There's a music, so it seems,
That assuages and redeems,
35   More than reason, more than dreams.

There's a music yet unheard
By the creature of the word,
Though it matters little more
Than a wave-wash on a shore—
40   Till a Demon shuts a door.

So, if he be very still
With his Demon, and one will,
Murmurs of it may be blown
To my friend who is alone
45   In a room that I have known.

THE POOR RELATION

No longer torn by what she knows
And sees within the eyes of others,
Her doubts are when the daylight goes,
Her fears are for the few she bothers.
5   She tells them it is wholly wrong
Of her to stay alive so long;
And when she smiles her forehead shows
A crinkle that had been her mother's.

Beneath her beauty, blanched with pain,
10   And wistful yet for being cheated,
A child would seem to ask again
A question many times repeated;
But no rebellion has betrayed
Her wonder at what she has paid
15   For memories that have no stain,
For triumph born to be defeated.

To those who come for what she was—
The few left who know where to find her—
She clings, for they are all she has;
20   And she may smile when they remind her,
As heretofore, of what they know
Of roses that are still to blow
By ways where not so much as grass
Remains of what she sees behind her.

25 They stay a while, and having done
What penance or the past requires,
They go, and leave her there alone
To count her chimneys and her spires.
Her lip shakes when they go away,
30 And yet she would not have them stay;
She knows as well as anyone
That Pity, having played, soon tires.

But one friend always reappears,
A good ghost, not to be forsaken;
35 Whereat she laughs and has no fears
Of what a ghost may reawaken,
But welcomes, while she wears and mends
The poor relation's odds and ends,
Her truant from a tomb of years—
40 Her power of youth so early taken.

Poor laugh, more slender than her song
It seems; and there are none to hear it
With even the stopped ears of the strong
For breaking heart or broken spirit.
45 The friends who clamored for her place,
And would have scratched her for her face,
Have lost her laughter for so long
That none would care enough to fear it.

None live who need fear anything
50 From her, whose losses are their pleasure;
The plover with a wounded wing
Stays not the flight that others measure;
So there she waits, and while she lives,
And death forgets, and faith forgives,
55 Her memories go foraging
For bits of childhood song they treasure.

And like a giant harp that hums
On always, and is always blending
The coming of what never comes
60 With what has past and had an ending,
The City trembles, throbs, and pounds
Outside, and through a thousand sounds
The small intolerable drums
Of Time are like slow drops descending.

65 Bereft enough to shame a sage
And given little to long sighing,
With no illusion to assuage
The lonely changelessness of dying,—
Unsought, unthought-of, and unheard,
70 She sings and watches like a bird,
Safe in a comfortable cage
From which there will be no more flying.

LLEWELLYN AND THE TREE

Could he have made Priscilla share
   The paradise that he had planned,
Llewellyn would have loved his wife
   As well as any in the land.

5   Could he have made Priscilla cease
   To goad him for what God left out,
Llewellyn would have been as mild
   As any we have read about.

Could all have been as all was not,
10   Llewellyn would have had no story;
He would have stayed a quiet man
   And gone his quiet way to glory.

But howsoever mild he was
   Priscilla was implacable;
15   And whatsoever timid hopes
   He built—she found them, and they fell.

And this went on, with intervals
   Of labored harmony between
Resounding discords, till at last
20   Llewellyn turned—as will be seen.

Priscilla, warmer than her name,
   And shriller than the sound of saws,
Pursued Llewellyn once too far,
   Not knowing quite the man he was.

25 The more she said, the fiercer clung
        The stinging garment of his wrath;
    And this was all before the day
        When Time tossed roses in his path.

    Before the roses ever came
30   Llewellyn had already risen.
    The roses may have ruined him,
        They may have kept him out of prison.

    And she who brought them, being Fate,
        Made roses do the work of spears,—
35 Though many made no more of her
        Than civet, coral, rouge, and years.

    You ask us what Llewellyn saw,
        But why ask what may not be given?
    To some will come a time when change
40   Itself is beauty, if not heaven.

    One afternoon Priscilla spoke,
        And her shrill history was done;
    At any rate, she never spoke
        Like that again to anyone.

45 One gold October afternoon
        Great fury smote the silent air;
    And then Llewellyn leapt and fled
        Like one with hornets in his hair.

    Llewellyn left us, and he said
50   Forever, leaving few to doubt him;
    And so, through frost and clicking leaves,
        The Tilbury way went on without him.

And slowly, through the Tilbury mist,
   The stillness of October gold
55   Went out like beauty from a face.
   Priscilla watched it, and grew old.

He fled, still clutching in his flight
   The roses that had been his fall;
The Scarlet One, as you surmise,
60   Fled with him, coral, rouge, and all.

Priscilla, waiting, saw the change
   Of twenty slow October moons;
And then she vanished, in her turn
   To be forgotten, like old tunes.

65   So they were gone—all three of them,
   I should have said, and said no more,
Had not a face once on Broadway
   Been one that I had seen before.

The face and hands and hair were old,
70   But neither time nor penury
Could quench within Llewellyn's eyes
   The shine of his one victory.

The roses, faded and gone by,
   Left ruin where they once had reigned;
75   But on the wreck, as on old shells,
   The color of the rose remained.

His fictive merchandise I bought
   For him to keep and show again,
Then led him slowly from the crush
80   Of his cold-shouldered fellow men.

"And so, Llewellyn," I began—
    "Not so," he said; "not so at all:
I've tried the world, and found it good,
    For more than twenty years this fall.

85 "And what the world has left of me
        Will go now in a little while."
    And what the world had left of him
        Was partly an unholy guile.

    "That I have paid for being calm
90   Is what you see, if you have eyes;
    For let a man be calm too long,
        He pays for much before he dies.

    "Be calm when you are growing old
        And you have nothing else to do;
95 Pour not the wine of life too thin
        If water means the death of you.

    "You say I might have learned at home
        The truth in season to be strong?
    Not so; I took the wine of life
100   Too thin, and I was calm too long.

    "Like others who are strong too late,
        For me there was no going back;
    For I had found another speed,
        And I was on the other track.

105 "God knows how far I might have gone
        Or what there might have been to see;
    But my speed had a sudden end,
        And here you have the end of me."

105

The end or not, it may be now
110   But little farther from the truth
To say those worn satiric eyes
    Had something of immortal youth.

He may among the millions here
    Be one; or he may, quite as well,
115 Be gone to find again the Tree
    Of Knowledge, out of which he fell.

He may be near us, dreaming yet
    Of unrepented rouge and coral;
Or in a grave without a name
120   May be as far off as a moral.

BEWICK FINZER

Time was when his half million drew
    The breath of six per cent;
But soon the worm of what-was-not
    Fed hard on his content;
5 And something crumbled in his brain
    When his half million went.

Time passed, and filled along with his
    The place of many more;
Time came, and hardly one of us
10   Had credence to restore,
From what appeared one day, the man
    Whom we had known before.

The broken voice, the withered neck,
    The coat worn out with care,
15 The cleanliness of indigence,
    The brilliance of despair,
The fond imponderable dreams
    Of affluence,—all were there.

Poor Finzer, with his dreams and schemes,
20   Fares hard now in the race,
With heart and eye that have a task
    When he looks in the face
Of one who might so easily
    Have been in Finzer's place.

25   He comes unfailing for the loan
       We give and then forget;
    He comes, and probably for years
       Will he be coming yet,—
    Familiar as an old mistake,
30   And futile as regret.

BOKARDO

Well, Bokardo, here we are;
    Make yourself at home.
Look around—you haven't far
    To look—and why be dumb?
5 Not the place that used to be,
Not so many things to see;
But there's room for you and me.
    And you—you've come.

Talk a little; or, if not,
10   Show me with a sign
Why it was that you forgot
    What was yours and mine.
Friends, I gather, are small things
In an age when coins are kings;
15 Even at that, one hardly flings
    Friends before swine.

Rather strong? I knew as much,
    For it made you speak.
No offense to swine, as such,
20   But why this hide-and-seek?
You have something on your side,
And you wish you might have died,
So you tell me. And you tried
    One night last week?

25 You tried hard? And even then
    Found a time to pause?

When you try as hard again,
   You'll have another cause.
When you find yourself at odds
30   With all dreamers of all gods,
You may smite yourself with rods—
   But not the laws.

Though they seem to show a spite
   Rather devilish,
35   They move on as with a might
   Stronger than your wish.
Still, however strong they be,
They bide man's authority:
Xerxes, when he flogged the sea,
40   May've scared a fish.

It's a comfort, if you like,
   To keep honor warm,
But as often as you strike
   The laws, you do no harm.
45   To the laws, I mean. To you—
That's another point of view,
One you may as well indue
   With some alarm.

Not the most heroic face
50   To present, I grant;
Nor will you insure disgrace
   By fearing what you want
Freedom has a world of sides,
And if reason once derides
55   Courage, then your courage hides
   A deal of cant.

Learn a little to forget
   Life was once a feast;
You aren't fit for dying yet,
   So don't be a beast.
Few men with a mind will say,
Thinking twice, that they can pay
Half their debts of yesterday,
   Or be released.

There's a debt now on your mind
   More than any gold?
And there's nothing you can find
   Out there in the cold?
Only—what's his name?—Remorse?
And Death riding on his horse?
Well, be glad there's nothing worse
   Than you have told.

Leave Remorse to warm his hands
   Outside in the rain.
As for Death, he understands,
   And he will come again.
Therefore, till your wits are clear,
Flourish and be quiet—here.
But a devil at each ear
   Will be a strain?

Past a doubt they will indeed,
   More than you have earned.
I say that because you need
   Ablution, being burned?
Well, if you must have it so,
Your last flight went rather low.
Better say you had to know
   What you have learned.

And that's over. Here you are,
90   Battered by the past.
Time will have his little scar,
        But the wound won't last.
Nor shall harrowing surprise
Find a world without its eyes
95   If a star fades when the skies
        Are overcast.

God knows there are lives enough,
        Crushed, and too far gone
Longer to make sermons of,
100   And those we leave alone.
Others, if they will, may rend
The worn patience of a friend
Who, though smiling, sees the end,
        With nothing done.

105   But your fervor to be free
        Fled the faith it scorned;
Death demands a decency
        Of you, and you are warned.
But for all we give we get
110   Mostly blows? Don't be upset;
You, Bokardo, are not yet
        Consumed or mourned.

There'll be falling into view
        Much to rearrange;
115   And there'll be a time for you
        To marvel at the change.
They that have the least to fear
Question hardest what is here;
When long-hidden skies are clear,
120   The stars look strange.

THE WANDERING JEW

I saw by looking in his eyes
That they remembered everything;
And this was how I came to know
That he was here, still wandering.
5   For though the figure and the scene
Were never to be reconciled,
I knew the man as I had known
His image when I was a child.

With evidence at every turn,
10   I should have held it safe to guess
That all the newness of New York
Had nothing new in loneliness;
Yet here was one who might be Noah,
Or Nathan, or Abimelech,
15   Or Lamech, out of ages lost,—
Or, more than all, Melchizedek.

Assured that he was none of these,
I gave them back their names again,
To scan once more those endless eyes
20   Where all my questions ended then.
I found in them what they revealed
That I shall not live to forget,
And wondered if they found in mine
Compasson that I might regret.

25 Pity, I learned, was not the least
Of time's offending benefits
That had now for so long impugned
The conservation of his wits:
Rather it was that I should yield,
30 Alone, the fealty that presents
The tribute of a tempered ear
To an untempered eloquence.

Before I pondered long enough
On whence he came and who he was,
35 I trembled at his ringing wealth
Of manifold anathemas;
I wondered, while he seared the world,
What new defection ailed the race,
And if it mattered how remote
40 Our fathers were from such a place.

Before there was an hour for me
To contemplate with less concern
The crumbling realms awaiting us
Then his that was beyond return,
45 A dawning on the dust of years
Had shaped with an elusive light
Mirages of remembered scenes
That were no longer for the sight.

For now the gloom that hid the man
50 Became a daylight on his wrath,
And one wherein my fancy viewed
New lions ramping in his path.
The old were dead and had no fangs,
Wherefore he loved them—seeing not
55 They were the same that in their time
had eaten everything they caught.

The world around him was a gift
Of anguish to his eyes and ears,
And one that he had long reviled
60 As fit for devils, not for seers.
Where, then, was there a place for him
That on this other side of death
Saw nothing good, as he had seen
No good come out of Nazareth?

65 Yet here there was a reticence,
And I believe his only one,
That hushed him as if he beheld
A Presence that would not be gone.
In such a silence he confessed
70 How much there was to be denied;
And he would look at me and live,
As others might have looked and died.

As if at last he knew again
That he had always known, his eyes
75 Were like to those of one who gazed
On those of One who never dies.
For such a moment he revealed
What life has in it to be lost;
And I could ask if what I saw,
80 Before me there, was man or ghost.

He may have died so many times
That all there was of him to see
Was pride, that kept itself alive
As too rebellious to be free;
85 He may have told, when more than once
Humility seemed imminent,
How many a lonely time in vain
The Second Coming came and went.

Whether he still defies or not
90 The failure of an angry task
That relegates him out of time
To chaos, I can only ask.
But as I knew him, so he was;
And somewhere among men to-day
95 Those old, unyielding eyes may flash,
And flinch—and look the other way.

THE MILL

The miller's wife had waited long,
    The tea was cold, the fire was dead;
And there might yet be nothing wrong
    In how he went and what he said:
5   "There are no millers any more,"
    Was all that she had heard him say;
And he had lingered at the door
    So long that it seemed yesterday.

Sick with a fear that had no form
10   She knew that she was there at last;
And in the mill there was a warm
    And mealy fragrance of the past.
What else there was would only seem
    To say again what he had meant;
15   And what was hanging from a beam
    Would not have heeded where she went.

And if she thought it followed her,
    She may have reasoned in the dark
That one way of the few there were
20   Would hide her and would leave no mark:
Black water, smooth above the weir
    Like starry velvet in the night,
Though ruffled once, would soon appear
    The same as ever to the sight.

THE DARK HILLS

Dark hills at evening in the west,
Where sunset hovers like a sound
Of golden horns that sang to rest
Old bones of warriors under ground,
5   Far now from all the bannered ways
Where flash the legions of the sun,
You fade—as if the last of days
Were fading, and all wars were done.

THE THREE TAVERNS

When the brethren heard of us, they came to meet us as far as
Appii Forum, and The Three Taverns.   (Acts xxviii, 15)

Herodion, Apelles, Amplias,
And Andronicus? Is it you I see—
At last? And is it you now that are gazing
As if in doubt of me? Was I not saying
5   That I should come to Rome? I did say that;
And I said furthermore that I should go
On westward, where the gateway of the world
Lets in the central sea. I did say that,
But I say only, now, that I am Paul—
10 A prisoner of the Law, and of the Lord
A voice made free. If there be time enough
To live, I may have more to tell you then
Of western matters. I go now to Rome,
Where Caesar waits for me, and I shall wait,
15 And Caesar knows how long. In Caesarea
There was a legend of Agrippa saying
In a light way to Festus, having heard
My deposition, that I might be free,
Had I stayed free of Caesar; but the word
20 Of God would have it as you see it is—
And here I am. The cup that I shall drink
Is mine to drink—the moment or the place
Not mine to say. If it be now in Rome,
Be it now in Rome; and if your faith exceed
25 The shadow cast of hope, say not of me
Too surely or too soon that years and shipwreck,

And all the many deserts I have crossed
That are not named or regioned, have undone
Beyond the brevities of our mortal healing
30   The part of me that is the least of me.
You see an older man than he who fell
Prone to the earth when he was nigh Damascus,
Where the great light came down; yet I am he
That fell, and he that saw, and he that heard.
35   And I am here, at last; and if at last
I give myself to make another crumb
For this pernicious feast of time and men—
Well, I have seen too much of time and men
To fear the ravening or the wrath of either.

40   Yes, it is Paul you see—the Saul of Tarsus
That was a fiery Jew, and had men slain
For saying Something was beyond the Law,
And in ourselves. I fed my suffering soul
Upon the Law till I went famishing,
45   Not knowing that I starved. How should I know,
More then than any, that the food I had—
What else it may have been—was not for me?
My fathers and their fathers and their fathers
Had found it good, and said there was no other,
50   And I was of the line. When Stephen fell,
Among the stones that crushed his life away,
There was no place alive that I could see
For such a man. Why should a man be given
To live beyond the Law? So I said then,
55   As men say now to me. How then do I
Persist in living? Is that what you ask?
If so, let my appearance be for you
No living answer; for Time writes of death
On men before they die, and what you see
60   Is not the man. The man that you see not—

The man within the man—is most alive;
Though hatred would have ended, long ago,
The bane of his activities. I have lived,
Because the faith within me that is life
65 Endures to live, and shall, till soon or late,
Death, like a friend unseen, shall say to me
My toil is over and my work begun.

How often, and how many a time again,
Have I said I should be with you in Rome!
70 He who is always coming never comes,
Or comes too late, you may have told yourselves;
And I may tell you now that after me,
Whether I stay for little or for long,
The wolves are coming. Have an eye for them,
75 And a more careful ear for their confusion
Than you need have much longer for the sound
Of what I tell you—should I live to say
More than I say to Caesar. What I know
Is down for you to read in what is written;
80 And if I cloud a little with my own
Mortality the gleam that is immortal,
I do it only because I am I—
Being on earth and of it, in so far
As time flays yet the remnant. This you know;
85 And if I sting men, as I do sometimes,
With a sharp word that hurts, it is because
Man's habit is to feel before he sees;
And I am of a race that feels. Moreover,
The world is here for what is not yet here
90 For more than are a few; and even in Rome,
Where men are so enamored of the Cross
That fame has echoed, and increasingly,
The music of your love and of your faith
To foreign ears that are as far away

As Antioch and Haran, yet I wonder
How much of love you know, and if your faith
Be the shut fruit of words. If so, remember
Words are but shells unfilled. Jews have at least
A Law to make them sorry they were born
If they go long without it; and these Gentiles,
For the first time in shrieking history,
Have love and law together, if so they will,
For their defense and their immunity
In these last days. Rome, if I know the name,
Will have anon a crown of thorns and fire
Made ready for the wreathing of new masters,
Of whom we are appointed, you and I,—
And you are still to be when I am gone,
Should I go presently. Let the word fall,
Meanwhile, upon the dragon-ridden field
Of circumstance, either to live or die;
Concerning which there is a parable,
Made easy for the comfort and attention
Of those who preach, fearing they preach in vain.
You are to plant, and then to plant again
Where you have gathered, gathering as you go;
For you are in the fields that are eternal,
And you have not the burden of the Lord
Upon your mortal shoulders. What you have
Is a light yoke, made lighter by the wearing,
Till it shall have the wonder and the weight
Of a clear jewel, shining with a light
Wherein the sun and all the fiery stars
May soon be fading. When Gamaliel said
That if they be of men these things are nothing
But if they be of God, they are for none
To overthrow, he spoke as a good Jew,
And one who stayed a Jew; and he said all.
And you know, by the temper of your faith,

130 How far the fire is in you that I felt
　　Before I knew Damascus. A word here,
　　Or there, or not there, or not anywhere,
　　Is not the Word that lives and is the life;
　　And you, therefore, need weary not yourselves
135 With jealous aches of others. If the world
　　Were not a world of aches and innovations,
　　Attainment would have no more joy of it.
　　There will be creeds and schisms, creeds in creeds,
　　And schisms in schisms; myriads will be done
140 To death because a farthing has two sides,
　　And is at last a farthing. Telling you this,
　　I, who bid men to live, appeal to Caesar.
　　Once I had said the ways of God were dark,
　　Meaning by that the dark ways of the Law.
145 Such is the Glory of our tribulations;
　　For the Law kills the flesh that kills the Law,
　　And we are then alive. We have eyes then;
　　And we have then the Cross between two worlds—
　　To guide us, or to blind us for a time,
150 Till we have eyes indeed. The fire that smites
　　A few on highways, changing all at once,
　　Is not for all. The power that holds the world
　　Away from God that holds himself away—
　　Farther away than all your works and words
155 Are like to fly without the wings of faith—
　　Was not, nor ever shall be, a small hazard
　　Enlivening the ways of easy leisure
　　Or the cold road of knowledge. When our eyes
　　Have wisdom, we see more than we remember;
160 And the old world of our captivities
　　May then become a smitten glimpse of ruin,
　　Like one where vanished hewers have had their day
　　Of wrath on Lebanon. Before we see,
　　Meanwhile, we suffer; and I come to you,

At last, through many storms and through much
        night.

        Yet whatsoever I have undergone,
        My keepers in this instance are not hard.
        But for the chance of an ingratitude,
        I might indeed be curious of their mercy,
170   And fearful of their leisure while I wait,
        A few leagues out of Rome. Men go to Rome,
        Not always to return—but not that now.
        Meanwhile, I seem to think you look at me
        With eyes that are at last more credulous
175   Of my identity. You remark in me
        No sort of leaping giant, though some words
        Of mine to you from Corinth may have leapt
        A little through your eyes into your soul.
        I trust they were alive, and are alive
180   Today; for there be none that shall indite
        So much of nothing as the man of words
        Who writes in the Lord's name for his name's sake
        And has not in his blood the fire of time
        To warm eternity. Let such a man—
185   If once the light is in him and endures—
        Content himself to be the general man,
        Set free to sift the decencies and thereby
        To learn, except he be one set aside
        For sorrow, more of pleasure than of pain;
190   Though if his light be not the light indeed,
        But a brief shine that never really was,
        And fails, leaving him worse than where he was,
        Then shall he be of all men destitute.
        And here were not an issue for much ink,
195   Or much offending faction among scribes.

The Kingdom is within us, we are told;
And when I say to you that we possess it
In such a measure as faith makes it ours,
I say it with a sinner's privilege
200 Of having seen and heard, and seen again,
After a darkness; and if I affirm
To the last hour that faith affords alone
The Kingdom entrance and an entertainment,
I do not see myself as one who says
205 To man that he shall sit with folded hands
Against the Coming. If I be anything,
I move a driven agent among my kind,
Establishing by the faith of Abraham,
And by the grace of their necessities,
210 The clamoring word that is the word of life
Nearer than heretofore to the solution
Of their tomb-serving doubts. If I have loosed
A shaft of language that has flown sometimes
A little higher than the hearts and heads
215 Of nature's minions, it will yet be heard,
Like a new song that waits for distant ears.
I cannot be the man that I am not;
And while I own that earth is my affliction,
I am a man of earth, who says not all
220 To all alike. That were impossible.
Even as it were so that He should plant
A larger garden first. But you today
Are for the larger sowing; and your seed,
A little mixed, will have, as He foresaw,
225 The foreign harvest of a wider growth,
And one without an end. Many there are,
And are to be, that shall partake of it,
Though none may share it with an understanding
That is not his alone. We are all alone;
230 And yet we are all parcelled of one order—

Jew, Gentile, or barbarian in the dark
Of wildernesses that are not so much
As names yet in a book. And there are many,
Finding at last that words are not the Word,
235 And finding only that, will flourish aloft,
Like heads of captured Pharisees on pikes,
Our contradictions and discrepancies;
And there are many more will hang themselves
Upon the letter, seeing not in the Word
240 The friend of all who fail, and in their faith
A sword of excellence to cut them down.

As long as there are glasses that are dark—
And there are many—we see darkly through them;
All which have I conceded and set down
245 In words that have no shadow. What is dark
Is dark, and we may not say otherwise;
Yet what may be as dark as a lost fire
For one of us, may still be for another
A coming gleam across the gulf of ages,
250 And a way home from shipwreck to the shore;
And so, through pangs and ills and desperations,
There may be light for all. There shall be light.
As much as that, you know. You cannot say
This woman or that man will be the next
255 On whom it falls; you are not here for that.
Your ministration is to be for others
The firing of a rush that may for them
Be soon the fire itself. The few at first
Are fighting for the multitude at last;
260 Therefore remember what Gamaliel said
Before you, when the sick were lying down
In streets all night for Peter's passing shadow.
Fight, and say what you feel; say more than words.
Give men to know that even their days of earth

265　To come are more than ages that are gone.
　　Say what you feel, while you have time to say it.
　　Eternity will answer for itself,
　　Without your intercession; yet the way
　　For many is a long one, and as dark,
270　Meanwhile, as dreams of hell. See not your toil
　　Too much, and if I be away from you
　　Think of me as a brother to yourselves,
　　Of many blemishes. Beware of stoics,
　　And give your left hand to grammarians;
275　And when you seem, as many a time you may,
　　To have no other friend than hope, remember
　　That you are not the first, or yet the last.

　　The best of life, until we see beyond
　　The shadows of ourselves (and they are less
280　Than even the blindest of indignant eyes
　　Would have them) is in what we do not know.
　　Make, then, for all your fears a place to sleep
　　With all your faded sins; nor think yourselves
　　Egregious and alone for your defects
285　Of youth and yesterday. I was young once;
　　And there's a question if you played the fool
　　With a more fervid and inherent zeal
　　Than I have in my story to remember,
　　Or gave your necks to folly's conquering foot,
290　Or flung yourselves with an unstudied aim,
　　More frequently than I. Never mind that.
　　Man's little house of days will hold enough,
　　Sometimes, to make him wish it were not his,
　　But it will not hold all. Things that are dead
295　Are best without it, and they own their death
　　By virtue of their dying. Let them go,—
　　But think you not the world is ashes yet,
　　And you have all the fire. The world is here

Today, and it may not be gone tomorrow;
300 For there are millions, and there may be more,
To make in turn a various estimation
Of its old ills and ashes, and the traps
Of its apparent wrath. Many with ears
That hear not yet, shall have ears given to them,
305 And then they shall hear strangely. Many with eyes
That are incredulous of the Mystery
Shall yet be driven to feel, and then to read
Where language has an end and is a veil,
Not woven of our words. Many that hate
310 Their kind are soon to know that without love
Their faith is but the perjured name of nothing.
I that have done some hating in my time
See now no time for hate; I that have left,
Fading behind me like familiar lights
315 That are to shine no more for my returning,
Home, friends, and honors,—I that have lost all else
For wisdom, and the wealth of it, say now
To you that out of wisdom has come love
That measures and is of itself the measure,
320 Of works and hope and faith. Your longest hours
Are not so long that you may torture them
And harass not yourselves; and the last days
Are on the way that you prepare for them,
And was prepared for you, here in a world
325 Where you have sinned and suffered, striven and seen.
If you be not so hot for counting them
Before they come that you consume yourselves,
Peace may attend you all in these last days—
And me, as well as you. Yes, even in Rome.

330 Well, I have talked and rested, though I fear
My rest has not been yours; in which event,
Forgive one who is only seven leagues

From Caesar. When I told you I should come,
I did not see myself the criminal
335 You contemplate, for seeing beyond the Law
That which the Law saw not. But this, indeed,
Was good of you, and I shall not forget;
No, I shall not forget you came so far
To meet a man so dangerous. Well, farewell.
340 They come to tell me I am going now—
With them. I hope that we shall meet again,
But none may say what he shall find in Rome.

DEMOS

I

All you that are enamored of my name
    And least intent on what most I require,
    Beware; for my design and your desire,
Deplorably, are not as yet the same.
5 Beware, I say, the failure and the shame
    Of losing that for which you now aspire
    So blindly, and of hazarding entire
The gift that I was bringing when I came.

Give as I will, I cannot give you sight
10   Whereby to see that with you there are some
    To lead you, and be led. But they are dumb
Before the wrangling and the shrill delight
    Of your deliverance that has not come,
And shall not, if I fail you—as I might.

II

15 So little have you seen of what awaits
    Your fevered glimpse of a democracy
    Confused and foiled with an equality
Not equal to the envy it creates,
That you see not how near you are the gates
20   Of an old king who listens fearfully
    To you that are outside and are to be
The noisy lords of imminent estates.

Rather be then your prayer that you shall have
    Your kingdom undishonored. Having all,
      See not the great among you for the small,
But hear their silence; for the few shall save
    The many, or the many are to fall—
Still to be wrangling in a noisy grave.

THE FLYING DUTCHMAN

Unyielding in the pride of his defiance,
  Afloat with none to serve or to command,
Lord of himself at last, and all by Science,
  He seeks the Vanished Land.

5 Alone, by the one light of his one thought,
  He steers to find the shore from which we came,
Fearless of in what coil he may be caught
  On seas that have no name.

Into the night he sails; and after night
10 There is a dawning, though there be no sun;
Wherefore, with nothing but himself in sight,
  Unsighted, he sails on.

At last there is a lifting of the cloud
  Between the flood before him and the sky;
15 And then—though he may curse the Power aloud
  That has no power to die—

He steers himself away from what is haunted
  By the old ghost of what has been before,—
Abandoning, as always, and undaunted,
20 One fog-walled island more.

TACT

Observant of the way she told
  So much of what was true,
No vanity could long withhold
  Regard that was her due:
She spared him the familiar guile,
  So easily achieved,
That only made a man to smile
  And left him undeceived.

Aware that all imagining
  Of more than what she meant
Would urge an end of everything,
  He stayed; and when he went,
They parted with a merry word
  That was to him as light
As any that was ever heard
  Upon a starry night.

She smiled a little, knowing well
  That he would not remark
The ruins of a day that fell
  Around her in the dark:
He saw no ruins anywhere,
  Nor fancied there were scars
On anyone who lingered there,
  Alone below the stars.

JOHN BROWN

Though for your sake I would not have you now
So near to me tonight as now you are,
God knows how much a stranger to my heart
Was any cold word that I may have written;
5   And you, poor woman that I made my wife,
You have had more of loneliness, I fear,
Than I—though I have been the most alone,
Even when the most attended. So it was
God set the mark of his inscrutable
10   Necessity on one that was to grope,
And serve, and suffer, and withal be glad
For what was his, and is, and is to be,
When his old bones, that are a burden now,
Are saying what the man who carried them
15   Had not the power to say. Bones in a grave,
Cover them as they will with choking earth,
May shout the truth to men who put them there,
More than all orators. And so, my dear,
Since you have cheated wisdom for the sake
20   Of sorrow, let your sorrow be for you,
This last of nights before the last of days,
The lying ghost of what there is of me
That is the most alive. There is no death
For me in what they do. Their death it is
25   They should heed most when the sun comes again
To make them solemn. There are some I know
Whose eyes will hardly see their occupation,
For tears in them—and all for one old man;

For some of them will pity this old man,
30 Who took upon himself the work of God
Because he pitied millions. That will be
For them, I fancy, their compassionate
Best way of saying what is best in them
To say; for they can say no more than that,
35 And they can do no more than what the dawn
Of one more day shall give them light enough
To do. But there are many days to be,
And there are many men to give their blood,
As I gave mine for them. May they come soon!

40 May they come soon, I say. And when they
          come,
May all that I have said unheard be heard,
Proving at last, or maybe not—no matter—
What sort of madness was the part of me
That made me strike, whether I found the mark
45 Or missed it. Meanwhile, I've a strange content,
A patience, and a vast indifference
To what men say of me and what men fear
To say. There was a work to be begun,
And when the Voice, that I have heard so long,
50 Announced as in a thousand silences
An end of preparation, I began
The coming work of death which is to be,
That life may be. There is no other way
Than the old way of war for a new land
55 That will not know itself and is tonight
A stranger to itself, and to the world
A more prodigious upstart among states
Than I was among men, and so shall be
Till they are told and told, and told again;
60 For men are children, waiting to be told,
And most of them are children all their lives.

The good God in his wisdom had them so,
That now and then a madman or a seer
May shake them out of their complacency
And shame them into deeds. The major file
See only what their fathers may have seen,
Or may have said they saw when they saw
    nothing.
I do not say it matters what they saw.
Now and again to some lone soul or other
God speaks, and there is hanging to be done,—
As once there was a burning of our bodies
Alive, albeit our souls were sorry fuel.
But now the fires are few, and we are poised
Accordingly, for the state's benefit,
A few still minutes between heaven and earth.
The purpose is, when they have seen enough
Of what it is that they are not to see,
To pluck me as an unripe fruit of treason,
And then to fling me back to the same earth
Of which they are, as I suppose, the flower—
Not given to know the riper fruit that waits
For a more comprehensive harvesting.

Yes, may they come, and soon. Again I say,
May they come soon!—before too many of them
Shall be the bloody cost of our defection.
When hell waits on the dawn of a new state,
Better it were that hell should not wait long,—
Or so it is I see it who should see
As far or farther into time tonight
Than they who talk and tremble for me now,
Or wish me to those everlasting fires
That are for me no fear. Too many fires
Have sought me out and seared me to the bone—
Thereby, for all I know, to temper me

95 For what was mine to do. If I did ill
What I did well, let men say I was mad;
Or let my name for ever be a question
That will not sleep in history. What men say
I was will cool no cannon, dull no sword,
100 Invalidate no truth. Meanwhile, I was;
And the long train is lighted that shall burn,
Though floods of wrath may drench it, and hot feet
May stamp it for a slight time into smoke
That shall blaze up again with growing speed,
105 Until at last a fiery crash will come
To cleanse and shake a wounded hemisphere,
And heal it of a long malignity
That angry time discredits and disowns.

Tonight there are men saying many things;
110 And some who see life in the last of me
Will answer first the coming call to death;
For death is what is coming, and then life.
I do not say again for the dull sake
Of speech what you have heard me say before,
115 But rather for the sake of all I am,
And all God made of me. A man to die
As I do must have done some other work
Than man's alone. I was not after glory,
But there was glory with me, like a friend,
120 Throughout those crippling years when friends
were few,
And fearful to be known by their own names
When mine was vilified for their approval.
Yet friends they are, and they did what was given
Their will to do; they could have done no more.
125 I was the one man mad enough, it seems,
To do my work; and now my work is over.
And you, my dear, are not to mourn for me,

Or for your sons, more than a soul should mourn
In Paradise, done with evil and with earth.
130 There is not much of earth in what remains
For you; and what there may be left of it
For your endurance you shall have at last
In peace, without the twinge of any fear
For my condition; for I shall be done
135 With plans and actions that have heretofore
Made your days long and your nights ominous
With darkness and the many distances
That were between us. When the silence comes,
I shall in faith be nearer to you then
140 Than I am now in fact. What you see now
Is only the outside of an old man,
Older than years have made him. Let him die,
And let him be a thing for little grief.
There was a time for service and he served;
145 And there is no more time for anything
But a short gratefulness to those who gave
Their scared allegiance to an enterprise
That has the name of treason—which will serve
As well as any other for the present.
150 There are some deeds of men that have no names,
And mine may like as not be one of them.
I am not looking far for names tonight.
The King of Glory was without a name
Until men gave Him one; yet there He was,
155 Before we found Him and affronted Him
With numerous ingenuities of evil,
Of which one, with His aid, is to be swept
And washed out of the world with fire and blood.

Once I believed it might have come to pass
160 With a small cost of blood; but I was dreaming—
Dreaming that I believed. The Voice I heard

When I left you behind me in the north,—
To wait there and to wonder and grow old
Of loneliness,—told only what was best,
165 And with a saving vagueness, I should know
Till I knew more. And had I known even then—
After grim years of search and suffering,
So many of them to end as they began—
After my sickening doubts and estimations
170 Of plans abandoned and of new plans vain—
After a weary delving everywhere
For men with every virtue but the Vision—
Could I have known, I say, before I left you
That summer morning, all there was to know—
175 Even unto the last consuming word
That would have blasted every mortal answer
As lightning would annihilate a leaf,
I might have trembled on that summer morning;
I might have wavered; and I might have failed.

180 And there are many among men today
To say of me that I had best have wavered.
So has it been, so shall it always be,
For those of us who give ourselves to die
Before we are so parcelled and approved
185 As to be slaughtered by authority.
We do not make so much of what they say
As they of what our folly says of us;
They give us hardly time enough for that,
And thereby we gain much by losing little.
190 Few are alive to-day with less to lose
Than I who tell you this, or more to gain;
And whether I speak as one to be destroyed
For no good end outside his own destruction,
Time shall have more to say than men shall hear
195 Between now and the coming of that harvest

Which is to come. Before it comes, I go—
By the short road that mystery makes long
For man's endurance of accomplishment.
I shall have more to say when I am dead.

THE FALSE GODS

"We are false and evanescent, and aware of our deceit,
From the straw that is our vitals to the clay that is our
     feet.
You may serve us if you must, and you shall have
     your wage of ashes,—
Though arrears due thereafter may be hard for you to
     meet.

5   "You may swear that we are solid, you may say that
         we are strong,
But we know that we are neither and we say that you
         are wrong;
You may find an easy worship in acclaiming our
         indulgence,
But your large admiration of us now is not for long.

"If your doom is to adore us with a doubt that's
         never still,
10 And you pray to see our faces—pray in earnest, and
         you will.
You may gaze at us and live, and live assured of our
         confusion:
For the False Gods are mortal, and are made for you
         to kill.

"And you may as well observe, while apprehensively
         at ease
With an Art that's inorganic and is anything you
         please,

15   That anon your newest ruin may lie crumbling
         unregarded,
     Like an old shrine forgotten in a forest of new trees.

     "Howsoever like no other be the mode you may
         employ,
     There's an order in the ages for the ages to enjoy;
     Though the temples you are shaping and the passions
         you are singing
20   Are a long way from Athens and a longer way from
         Troy.

     "When we promise more than ever of what never shall
         arrive,
     And you seem a little more than ordinarily alive,
     Make a note that you are sure you understand our
         obligations—
     For there's grief always auditing where two and two
         are five.

25   "There was this for us to say and there was this for
         you to know,
     Though it humbles and it hurts us when we have to
         tell you so
     If you doubt the only truth in all our perjured
         composition,
     May the True Gods attend you and forget us when
         we go."

ARCHIBALD'S EXAMPLE

Old Archibald, in his eternal chair,
Where trespassers, whatever their degree,
Were soon frowned out again, was looking off
Across the clover when he said to me:

5 "My green hill yonder, where the sun goes down
Without a scratch, was once inhabited
By trees that injured him—an evil trash
That made a cage, and held him while he bled.

"Gone fifty years, I see them as they were
10 Before they fell. They were a crooked lot
To spoil my sunset, and I saw no time
In fifty years for crooked things to rot.

"Trees, yes; but not a service or a joy
To God or man, for they were thieves of light.
15 So down they came. Nature and I looked on,
And we were glad when they were out of sight.

"Trees are like men, sometimes; and that being so,
So much for that." He twinkled in his chair,
And looked across the clover to the place
20 That he remembered when the trees were there.

LAZARUS

"No, Mary, there was nothing—not a word.
Nothing, and always nothing. Go again
Yourself, and he may listen—or at least
Look up at you, and let you see his eyes.
5 I might as well have been the sound of rain,
A wind among the cedars, or a bird;
Or nothing. Mary, make him look at you;
And even if he should say that we are nothing,
To know that you have heard him will be something.
10 And yet he loved us, and it was for love
The Master gave him back. Why did he wait
So long before he came? Why did he weep?
I thought he would be glad—and Lazarus—
To see us all again as he had left us—
15 All as it was, all as it was before."

Mary, who felt her sister's frightened arms
Like those of someone drowning who had seized her,
Fearing at last they were to fail and sink
Together in this fog-stricken sea of strangeness,
20 Fought sadly, with bereaved indignant eyes,
To find again the fading shores of home
That she had seen but now could see no longer
Now she could only gaze into the twilight,
And in the dimness know that he was there,
25 Like someone that was not. He who had been
Their brother, and was dead, now seemed alive
Only in death again—or worse than death;

For tombs at least, always until today,
Though sad were certain. There was nothing certain
30   For man or God in such a day as this;
For there they were alone, and there was he—
Alone; and somewhere out of Bethany,
The Master—who had come to them so late,
Only for love of them and then so slowly,
35   And was for their sake hunted now by men
Who feared Him as they feared no other prey—
For the world's sake was hidden. "Better the tomb
For Lazarus than life, if this be life,"
She thought; and then to Martha, "No, my dear,"
40   She said aloud; "not as it was before.
Nothing is ever as it was before,
Where Time has been. Here there is more than Time;
And we that are so lonely and so far
From home, since he is with us here again,
45   Are farther now from him and from ourselves
Than we are from the stars. He will not speak
Until the spirit that is in him speaks;
And we must wait for all we are to know,
Or even to learn that we are not to know.
50   Martha, we are too near to this for knowledge,
And that is why it is that we must wait.
Our friends are coming if we call for them,
And there are covers we'll put over him
To make him warmer. We are too young, perhaps,
55   To say that we know better what is best
Than he. We do not know how old he is.
If you remember what the Master said,
Try to believe that we need have no fear.
Let me, the selfish and the careless one,
60   Be housewife and a mother for tonight;
For I am not so fearful as you are,
And I was not so eager."

Martha sank
Down at her sister's feet and there sat watching
65   A flower that had a small familiar name
That was as old as memory, but was not
The name of what she saw now in its brief
And infinite mystery that so frightened her
That life became a terror. Tears again
70   Flooded her eyes and overflowed. "No, Mary,"
She murmured slowly, hating her own words
Before she heard them, "you are not so eager
To see our brother as we see him now;
Neither is he who gave him back to us.
75   I was to be the simple one, as always,
And this was all for me." She stared again
Over among the trees where Lazarus,
Who seemed to be a man who was not there,
Might have been one more shadow among shadows,
80   If she had not remembered. Then she felt
The cool calm hands of Mary on her face,
And shivered, wondering if such hands were real.

"The Master loved you as he loved us all,
Martha; and you are saying only things
85   That children say when they have had no sleep.
Try somehow now to rest a little while;
You know that I am here, and that our friends
Are coming if I call."

Martha at last
90   Arose, and went with Mary to the door,
Where they stood looking off at the same place,
And at the same shape that was always there
As if it would not ever move or speak,
And always would be there. "Mary, go now,
95   Before the dark that will be coming hides him.

I am afraid of him out there alone,
Unless I see him; and I have forgotten
What sleep is. Go now—make him look at you—
And I shall hear him if he stirs or whispers.
100 Go!—or I'll scream and bring all Bethany
To come and make him speak. Make him say once
That he is glad, and God may say the rest.
Though He say I shall sleep, and sleep for ever,
I shall not care for that . . . Go!"

105   Mary, moving
Almost as if an angry child had pushed her,
Went forward a few steps; and having waited
As long as Martha's eyes would look at hers,
Went forward a few more, and a few more;
110 And so, until she came to Lazarus,
Who crouched with his face hidden in his hands,
Like one that had no face. Before she spoke,
Feeling her sister's eyes that were behind her
As if the door where Martha stood were now
115 As far from her as Egypt, Mary turned
Once more to see that she was there. Then, softly,
Fearing him not so much as wondering
What his first word might be, said, "Lazarus,
Forgive us if we seemed afraid of you;"
120 And having spoken, pitied her poor speech
That had so little seeming gladness in it,
So little comfort, and so little love.

There was no sign from him that he had heard,
Or that he knew that she was there, or cared
125 Whether she spoke to him again or died
There at his feet. "We love you, Lazarus,
And we are not afraid. The Master said
We need not be afraid. Will you not say

To me that you are glad? Look, Lazarus!
130   Look at my face, and see me. This is Mary."

She found his hands and held them. They were cool,
Like hers, but they were not so calm as hers.
Through the white robes in which his friends had
        wrapped him
When he had groped out of that awful sleep,
135   She felt him trembling and she was afraid.
At last he sighed; and she prayed hungrily
To God that she might hear again the voice
Of Lazarus, whose hands were giving her now
The recognition of a living pressure
140   That was almost a language. When he spoke,
Only one word that she had waited for
Came from his lips, and that word was her name.

"I heard them saying, Mary, that he wept
Before I woke." The words were low and shaken,
145   Yet Mary knew that he who uttered them
Was Lazarus; and that would be enough
Until there should be more . . . "Who made him
        come,
That he should weep for me? . . . Was it you, Mary?"
The questions held in his incredulous eyes
150   Were more than she would see. She looked away;
But she had felt them and should feel for ever,
She thought, their cold and lonely desperation
That had the bitterness of all cold things
That were not cruel. "I should have wept," he said,
155   "If I had been the Master. . . ."

                                Now she could feel
His hands above her hair—the same black hair
That once he made a jest of, praising it,

148

While Martha's busy eyes had left their work
160 To flash with laughing envy. Nothing of that
Was to be theirs again; and such a thought
Was like the flying by of a quick bird
Seen through a shadowy doorway in the twilight.
For now she felt his hands upon her head,
165 Like weights of kindness: "I forgive you, Mary. . . .
You did not know—Martha could not have known—
Only the Master knew. . . . Where is he now?
Yes, I remember. They came after him.
May the good God forgive him. . . . I forgive him.
170 I must; and I may know only from him
The burden of all this . . . Martha was here—
But I was not yet here. She was afraid. . . .
Why did he do it, Mary? Was it—you?
Was it for you? . . . Where are the friends I saw?
175 Yes, I remember. They all went away.
I made them go away. . . . Where is he now? . . .
What do I see down there? Do I see Martha—
Down by the door? . . . I must have time for this."

Lazarus looked about him fearfully,
180 And then again at Mary, who discovered
Awakening apprehension in his eyes,
And shivered at his feet. All she had feared
Was here; and only in the slow reproach
Of his forgiveness lived his gratitude.
185 Why had he asked if it was all for her
That he was here? And what had Martha meant?
Why had the Master waited? What was coming
To Lazarus, and to them, that had not come?
What had the Master seen before he came,
190 That he had come so late?

                              "Where is he, Mary?"
Lazarus asked again. "Where did he go?"
Once more he gazed about him, and once more
At Mary for an answer. "Have they found him?
195   Or did he go away because he wished
Never to look into my eyes again? . . .
That, I could understand. . . . Where is he, Mary?"

      "I do not know," she said. "Yet in my heart
I know that he is living, as you are living—
200   Living, and here. He is not far from us.
He will come back to us and find us all—
Lazarus, Martha, Mary—everything—
All as it was before. Martha said that.
And he said we were not to be afraid."
205   Lazarus closed his eyes while on his face
A tortured adumbration of a smile
Flickered an instant. "All as it was before,"
He murmured wearily. "Martha said that;
And he said you were not to be afraid . . .
210   Not you . . . Not you . . . Why should you be afraid?
Give all your little fears, and Martha's with them,
To me; and I will add them unto mine,
Like a few rain-drops to Gennesaret."

      "If you had frightened me in other ways,
215   Not willing it," Mary said, "I should have known
You still for Lazarus. But who is this?
Tell me again that you are Lazarus;
And tell me if the Master gave to you
No sign of a new joy that shall be coming
220   To this house that he loved. Are you afraid?
Are you afraid, who have felt everything—
And seen . . . ?"

But Lazarus only shook his head,
Staring with his bewildered shining eyes
225 Hard into Mary's face. "I do not know,
Mary," he said, and after a long time,
"When I came back, I knew the Master's eyes
Were looking into mine. I looked at his,
And there was more in them than I could see.
230 At first I could see nothing but his eyes;
Nothing else anywhere was to be seen—
Only his eyes. And they looked into mine—
Long into mine, Mary, as if he knew."

Mary began to be afraid of words
235 As she had never been afraid before
Of loneliness or darkness, or of death,
But now she must have more of them or die:
"He cannot know that there is worse than death,"
She said. "And you . . ."

240   "Yes, there is worse than death."
Said Lazarus; "and that was what he knew;
And that is what it was that I could see
This morning in his eyes. I was afraid,
But not as you are. There is worse than death,
245 Mary; and there is nothing that is good
For you in dying while you are still here.
Mary, never go back to that again.
You would not hear me if I told you more,
For I should say it only in a language
250 That you are not to learn by going back.
To be a child again is to go forward—
And that is much to know. Many grow old,
And fade, and go away, not knowing how much
That is to know. Mary, the night is coming,

255 And there will soon be darkness all around you.
Let us go down where Martha waits for us,
And let there be light shining in this house."

He rose, but Mary would not let him go:
"Martha, when she came back from here, said only
260 That she heard nothing. And have you no more
For Mary now than you had then for Martha?
Is Nothing, Lazarus, all you have for me?
Was Nothing all you found where you have been?
If that be so, what is there worse than that—
265 Or better—if that be so? And why should you,
With even our love, go the same dark road over?"

"I could not answer that, if that were so,"
Said Lazarus,—"not even if I were God.
Why should He care whether I came or stayed,
270 If that were so? Why should the Master weep—
For me, or for the world,—or save himself
Longer for nothing? And if that were so,
Why should a few years' more mortality
Make him a fugitive where flight were needless,
275 Had he but held his peace and given his nod
To an old Law that would be new as any?
I cannot say the answer to all that;
Though I may say that he is not afraid,
And that it is not for the joy there is
280 In serving an eternal Ignorance
Of our futility that he is here.
Is that what you and Martha mean by Nothing?
Is that what you are fearing? If that be so,
There are more weeds than lentils in your garden.
285 And one whose weeds are laughing at his harvest
May as well have no garden; for not there
Shall he be gleaning the few bits and orts

152

Of life that are to save him. For my part,
I am again with you, here among shadows
290 That will not always be so dark as this;
Though now I see there's yet an evil in me
That made me let you be afraid of me.
No, I was not afraid—not even of life.
I thought I was . . . I must have time for this;
295 And all the time there is will not be long.
I cannot tell you what the Master saw
This morning in my eyes. I do not know.
I cannot yet say how far I have gone,
Or why it is that I am here again,
300 Or where the old road leads. I do not know.
I know that when I did come back, I saw
His eyes again among the trees and faces—
Only his eyes; and they looked into mine—
Long into mine—long, long, as if he knew."

MR. FLOOD'S PARTY

Old Eben Flood, climbing alone one night
Over the hill between the town below
And the forsaken upland hermitage
That held as much as he should ever know
On earth again of home, paused warily.
The road was his with not a native near;
And Eben, having leisure, said aloud,
For no man else in Tilbury Town to hear:

"Well, Mr. Flood, we have the harvest moon
Again, and we may not have many more;
The bird is on the wing, the poet says,
And you and I have said it here before.
Drink to the bird." He raised up to the light
The jug that he had gone so far to fill,
And answered huskily: "Well, Mr. Flood,
Since you propose it, I believe I will."

Alone, as if enduring to the end
A valiant armor of scarred hopes outworn,
He stood there in the middle of the road
Like Roland's ghost winding a silent horn.
Below him, in the town among the trees,
Where friends of other days had honored him,
A phantom salutation of the dead
Rang thinly till old Eben's eyes were dim.

25 Then, as a mother lays her sleeping child
Down tenderly, fearing it may awake,
He set the jug down slowly at his feet
With trembling care, knowing that most things break;
And only when assured that on firm earth
30 It stood, as the uncertain lives of men
Assuredly did not, he paced away,
And with his hand extended paused again:

"Well, Mr. Flood, we have not met like this
In a long time; and many a change has come
35 To both of us, I fear, since last it was
We had a drop together. Welcome home!"
Convivially returning with himself,
Again he raised the jug up to the light;
And with an acquiescent quaver said:
40 "Well, Mr. Flood, if you insist, I might.

"Only a very little, Mr. Flood—
For auld lang syne. No more, sir; that will do."
So, for the time, apparently it did,
And Eben evidently thought so too;
45 For soon amid the silver loneliness
Of night he lifted up his voice and sang,
Secure, with only two moons listening,
Until the whole harmonious landscape rang—

"For auld lang syne." The weary throat gave out,
50 The last word wavered, and the song was done.
He raised again the jug regretfully
And shook his head, and was again alone.
There was not much that was ahead of him,
And there was nothing in the town below—
55 Where strangers would have shut the many doors
That many friends had opened long ago.

BEN TROVATO

The deacon thought. "I know them," he began,
"And they are all you ever heard of them—
Allurable to no sure theorem,
The scorn or the humility of man.
5 You say 'Can I believe it?'—and I can;
And I'm unwilling even to condemn
The benefaction of a stratagem
Like hers—and I'm a Presbyterian.

"Though blind, with but a wandering hour to live,
10 He felt the other woman in the fur
That now the wife had on. Could she forgive
All that? Apparently. Her rings were gone,
Of course; and when he found that she had none,
He smiled—as he had never smiled at her."

THE TREE IN PAMELA'S GARDEN

Pamela was too gentle to deceive
Her roses. "Let the men stay where they are,"
She said, "and if Apollo's avatar
Be one of them, I shall not have to grieve."
5   And so she made all Tilbury Town believe
She sighed a little more for the North Star
Than over men, and only in so far
As she was in a garden was like Eve.

Her neighbors—doing all that neighbors can
10 To make romance of reticence meanwhile—
Seeing that she had never loved a man,
Wished Pamela had a cat, or a small bird,
And only would have wondered at her smile
Could they have seen that she had overheard.

VAIN GRATUITIES

Never was there a man much uglier
In eyes of other women, or more grim:
"The Lord has filled her chalice to the brim,
So let us pray she's a philosopher,"
They said; and there was more they said of her—
Deeming it, after twenty years with him,
No wonder that she kept her figure slim
And always made you think of lavender.

But she, demure as ever, and as fair,
Almost, as they remembered her before
She found him, would have laughed had she been
    there;
And all they said would have been heard no more
Than foam that washes on an island shore
Where there are none to listen or to care.

LOST ANCHORS

Like a dry fish flung inland far from shore,
There lived a sailor, warped and ocean-browned,
Who told of an old vessel, harbor-drowned
And out of mind a century before,
Where divers, on descending to explore
A legend that had lived its way around
The world of ships, in the dark hulk had found
Anchors, which had been seized and seen no more.

Improving a dry leisure to invest
Their misadventure with a manifest
Analogy that he may read who runs,
The sailor made it old as ocean grass—
Telling of much that once had come to pass
With him, whose mother should have had no sons.

RECALLED

Long after there were none of them alive
About the place—where there is now no place
But a walled hole where fruitless vines embrace
Their parent skeletons that yet survive
In evil thorns—none of us could arrive
At a more cogent answer to their ways
Than one old Isaac in his latter days
Had humor or compassion to contrive.

I mentioned them, and Isaac shook his head:
"The Power that you call yours and I call mine
Extinguished in the last of them a line
That Satan would have disinherited.
When we are done with all but the Divine,
We die." And there was no more to be said.

MODERNITIES

Small knowledge have we that by knowledge met
May not some day be quaint as any told
In almagest or chronicle of old,
Whereat we smile because we are as yet
5   The last—though not the last who may forget
What cleavings and abrasions manifold
Have marked an armor that was never scrolled
Before for human glory and regret.

With infinite unseen enemies in the way
10   We have encountered the intangible,
To vanquish where our fathers, who fought well,
Scarce had assumed endurance for a day;
Yet we shall have our darkness, even as they,
And there shall be another tale to tell.

AFTERTHOUGHTS

We parted where the old gas-lamp still burned
Under the wayside maple and walked on,
Into the dark, as we had always done;
And I, no doubt, if he had not returned,
5 Might yet be unaware that he had earned
More than earth gives to many who have won
More than it has to give when they are gone—
As duly and indelibly I learned.

The sum of all that he came back to say
10 Was little then, and would be less today:
With him there were no Delphic heights to climb,
Yet his were somehow nearer the sublime.
He spoke, and went again by the old way—
Not knowing it would be for the last time.

CAPUT MORTUUM

Not even if with a wizard force I might
Have summoned whomsoever I would name,
Should anyone else have come than he who came,
Uncalled, to share with me my fire that night;
5   For though I should have said that all was right,
Or right enough, nothing had been the same
As when I found him there before the flame,
Always a welcome and a useful sight.

Unfailing and exuberant all the time,
10   Having no gold he paid with golden rhyme,
Of older coinage than his old defeat,
A debt that like himself was obsolete
In Art's long hazard, where no man may choose
Whether he play to win or toil to lose.

MONADNOCK THROUGH
THE TREES

Before there was in Egypt any sound
Of those who reared a more prodigious means
For the self-heavy sleep of kings and queens
Than hitherto had mocked the most renowned,—
5   Unvisioned here and waiting to be found,
Alone, amid remote and older scenes,
You loomed above ancestral evergreens
Before there were the first of us around.

And when the last of us, if we know how,
10 See farther from ourselves than we do now,
Assured with other sight than heretofore
That we have done our mortal best and worst,—
Your calm will be the same as when the first
Assyrians went howling south to war.

MANY ARE CALLED

The Lord Apollo, who has never died,
Still holds alone his immemorial reign,
Supreme in an impregnable domain
That with his magic he has fortified;
5   And though melodious multitudes have tried
In ecstasy, in anguish, and in vain,
With invocation sacred and profane
To lure him, even the loudest are outside.

Only at unconjectured intervals,
10   By will of him on whom no man may gaze,
By word of him whose law no man has read,
A questing light may rift the sullen walls,
To cling where mostly its infrequent rays
Fall golden on the patience of the dead.

REMBRANDT TO REMBRANDT

(Amsterdam, 1645)

And there you are again, now as you are.
Observe yourself as you discern yourself
In your discredited ascendency;
Without your velvet or your feathers now,
5 Commend your new condition to your fate,
And your conviction to the sieves of time.
Meanwhile appraise yourself, Rembrandt van Ryn,
Now as you are—formerly more or less
Distinguished in the civil scenery,
10 And once a painter. There you are again,
Where you may see that you have on your shoulders
No lovelier burden for an ornament
Than one man's head that's yours. Praise be to God
That you have that; for you are like enough
15 To need it now, my friend, and from now on;
For there are shadows and obscurities
Immediate or impending on your view,
That may be worse than you have ever painted
For the bewildered and unhappy scorn
20 Of injured Hollanders in Amsterdam
Who cannot find their fifty florins' worth
Of Holland face where you have hidden it
In your new golden shadow that excites them,
Or see that when the Lord made color and light
25 He made not one thing only, or believe
That shadows are not nothing. Saskia said,
Before she died, how they would swear at you,

And in commiseration at themselves.
She laughed a little, too, to think of them—
30 And then at me. . . . That was before she died.

And I could wonder, as I look at you,
There as I have you now, there as you are,
Or nearly so as any skill of mine
Has ever caught you in a bilious mirror,—
35 Yes, I could wonder long, and with a reason,
If all but everything achievable
In me were not achieved and lost already,
Like a fool's gold. But you there in the glass,
And you there on the canvas, have a sort
40 Of solemn doubt about it; and that's well
For Rembrandt and for Titus. All that's left
Of all that was is here; and all that's here
Is one man who remembers, and one child
Beginning to forget. One, two, and three,
45 The others died, and then—then Saskia died;
And then, so men believe, the painter died.
So men believe. So it all comes at once.
And here's a fellow painting in the dark,—
A loon who cannot see that he is dead
50 Before God lets him die. He paints away
At the impossible, so Holland has it,
For venom or for spite, or for defection,
Or else for God knows what. Well, if God knows,
And Rembrandt knows, it matters not so much
55 What Holland knows or cares. If Holland wants
Its heads all in a row, and all alike,
There's Franz to do them and to do them well—
Rat-catchers, archers, or apothecaries,
And one as like a rabbit as another.
60 Value received, and every Dutchman happy.
All's one to Franz, and to the rest of them,—

Their ways being theirs, are theirs.—But you, my
  friend,
If I have made you something as you are,
Will need those jaws and eyes and all the fight
65 And fire that's in them, and a little more,
To take you on and the world after you;
For now you fare alone, without the fashion
To sing you back and fling a flower or two
At your accusing feet. Poor Saskia saw
70 This coming that has come, and with a guile
Of kindliness that covered half her doubts
Would give me gold, and laugh . . . before she died.

And if I see the road that you are going,
You that are not so jaunty as aforetime,
75 God knows if she were not appointed well
To die. She might have wearied of it all
Before the worst was over, or begun.
A woman waiting on a man's avouch
Of the invisible, may not wait always
80 Without a word betweenwhiles, or a dash
Of poison on his faith. Yes, even she.
She might have come to see at last with others,
And then to say with others, who say more,
That you are groping on a phantom trail
85 Determining a dusky way to nowhere;
That errors unconfessed and obstinate
Have teemed and cankered in you for so long
That even your eyes are sick, and you see light
Only because you dare not see the dark
90 That is around you and ahead of you.
She might have come, by ruinous estimation
Of old applause and outworn vanities,
To clothe you over in a shroud of dreams,
And so be nearer to the counterfeit

95 Of her invention than aware of yours.
    She might, as well as any, by this time,
    Unwillingly and eagerly have bitten
    Another devil's-apple of unrest,
    And so, by some attendant artifice
100 Or other, might anon have had you sharing
    A taste that would have tainted everything,
    And so had been for two, instead of one,
    The taste of death in life—which is the food
    Of art that has betrayed itself alive
105 And is a food of hell. She might have heard
    Unhappily the temporary noise
    Of louder names than yours, and on frail urns
    That hardly will ensure a dwelling-place
    For even the dust that may be left of them,
110 She might, and angrily, as like as not,
    Look soon to find your name, not finding it.
    She might, like many another born for joy
    And for sufficient fulness of the hour,
    Go famishing by now, and in the eyes
115 Of pitying friends and dwindling satellites
    Be told of no uncertain dereliction
    Touching the cold offence of my decline.
    And even if this were so, and she were here
    Again to make a fact of all my fancy,
120 How should I ask of her to see with me
    Through night where many a time I seem in vain
    To seek for new assurance of a gleam
    That comes at last, and then, so it appears,
    Only for you and me—and a few more,
125 Perchance, albeit their faces are not many
    Among the ruins that are now around us.
    That was a fall, my friend, we had together—
    Or rather it was my house, mine alone,
    That fell, leaving you safe. Be glad for that.

130 There's life in you that shall outlive my clay
That's for a time alive and will in time
Be nothing—but not yet. You that are there
Where I have painted you are safe enough,
Though I see dragons. Verily, that was a fall—
135 A dislocating fall, a blinding fall,
A fall indeed. But there are no bones broken;
And even the teeth and eyes that I make out
Among the shadows, intermittently,
Show not so firm in their accoutrement
140 Of terror-laden unreality
As you in your neglect of their performance,—
Though for their season we must humor them
For what they are: devils undoubtedly,
But not so perilous and implacable
145 In their undoing of poor human triumph
As easy fashion—or brief novelty
That ails even while it grows, and like sick fruit
Falls down anon to an indifferent earth
To break with inward rot. I say all this,
150 And I concede, in honor of your silence,
A waste of innocent facility
In tints of other colors than are mine.
I cannot paint with words, but there's a time
For most of us when words are all we have
155 To serve our stricken souls. And here you say,
"Be careful, or you may commit your soul
Soon to the very devil of your denial."
I might have wagered on you to say that,
Knowing that I believe in you too surely
160 To spoil you with a kick or paint you over.

No, my good friend, Mynheer Rembrandt van Ryn—
Sometime a personage in Amsterdam,
But now not much—I shall not give myself

To be the sport of any dragon-spawn
165 Of Holland, or elsewhere. Holland was hell
Not long ago, and there were dragons then
More to be fought than any of these we see
That we may foster now. They are not real,
But not for that the less to be regarded;
170 For there are slimy tyrants born of nothing
That harden slowly into seeming life
And have the strength of madness. I confess,
Accordingly, the wisdom of your care
That I look out for them. Whether I would
175 Or not, I must; and here we are as one
With our necessity. For though you loom
A little harsh in your respect of time
And circumstance, and of ordained eclipse,
We know together of a golden flood
180 That with its overflow shall drown away
The dikes that held it; and we know thereby
That in its rising light there lives a fire
No devils that are lodging here in Holland
Shall put out wholly, or much agitate,
185 Except in unofficial preparation
They put out first the sun. It's well enough
To think of them; wherefore I thank you, sir,
Alike for your remembrance and attention.

But there are demons that are longer-lived
190 Than doubts that have a brief and evil term
To congregate among the futile shards
And architraves of eminent collapse.
They are a many-favored family,
All told, with not a misbegotten dwarf
195 Among the rest that I can love so little
As one occult abortion in especial
Who perches on a picture (when it's done)

And says, "What of it, Rembrandt, if you do?"
This incubus would seem to be a sort
200   Of chorus, indicating, for our good,
The silence of the few friends that are left:
"What of it, Rembrandt, even if you know?"
It says again; "and you don't know for certain.
What if in fifty or a hundred years
205   They find you out? You may have gone meanwhile
So greatly to the dogs that you'll not care
Much what they find. If this be all you are—
This unaccountable aspiring insect—
You'll sleep as easy in oblivion
210   As any sacred monk or parricide;
And if, as you conceive, you are eternal,
Your soul may laugh, remembering (if a soul
Remembers) your befrenzied aspiration
To smear with certain ochres and some oil
215   A few more perishable ells of cloth,
And once or twice, to square your vanity,
Prove it was you alone that should achieve
A mortal eye—that may, no less, tomorrow
Show an immortal reason why today
220   Men see no more. And what's a mortal eye
More than a mortal herring, who has eyes
As well as you? Why not paint herrings, Rembrandt?
Or if not herrings, why not a split beef?
Perceive it only in its unalloyed
225   Integrity, and you may find in it
A beautified accomplishment no less
Indigenous than one that appertains
To gentlemen and ladies eating it.
The same God planned and made you, beef and
        human:
230   And one, but for His whim, might be the other."

That's how he says it, Rembrandt, if you listen;
He says it, and he goes. And then, sometimes,
There comes another spirit in his place—
One with a more engaging argument,
235 And with a softer note for saying truth
Not soft. Whether it be the truth or not,
I name it so; for there's a string in me
Somewhere that answers—which is natural,
Since I am but a living instrument
240 Played on by powers that are invisible.
"You might go faster, if not quite so far,"
He says, "if in your vexed economy
There lived a faculty for saying yes
And meaning no, and then for doing neither;
245 But since Apollo sees it otherwise,
Your Dutchmen, who are swearing at you still
For your pernicious filching of their florins,
May likely curse you down their generation,
Not having understood there was no malice
250 Or grinning evil in a golden shadow
That shall outshine their slight identities
And hold their faces when their names are nothing.
But this, as you discern, or should by now
Surmise, for you is neither here nor there:
255 You made your picture as your demon willed it;
That's about all of that. Now make as many
As may be to be made,—for so you will,
Whatever the toll may be, and hold your light
So that you see, without so much to blind you
260 As even the cobweb-flash of a misgiving,
Assured and certain that if you see right
Others will have to see—albeit their seeing
Shall irk them out of their serenity
For such a time as umbrage may require.

265 But there are many reptiles in the night
That now is coming on, and they are hungry;
And there's a Rembrandt to be satisfied
Who never will be, howsoever much
He be assured of an ascendency
270 That has not yet a shadow's worth of sound
Where Holland has its ears. And what of that?
Have you the weary leisure or sick wit
That breeds of its indifference a false envy
That is the vermin on accomplishment?
275 Are you inaugurating your new service
With fasting for a food you would not eat?
You are the servant, Rembrandt, not the master,—
But you are not assigned with other slaves
That in their freedom are the most in fear.
280 One of the few that are so fortunate
As to be told their task and to be given
A skill to do it with a tool too keen
For timid safety, bow your elected head
Under the stars tonight, and whip your devils
285 Each to his nest in hell. Forget your days,
And so forgive the years that may not be
So many as to be more than you may need
For your particular consistency
In your peculiar folly. You are counting
290 Some fewer years than forty at your heels;
And they have not pursued your gait so fast
As your oblivion—which has beaten them,
And rides now on your neck like an old man
With iron shins and fingers. Let him ride
295 (You haven't so much to say now about that),
And in a proper season let him run.
You may be dead then, even as you may now
Anticipate some other mortal strokes
Attending your felicity; and for that,

300 Oblivion heretofore has done some running
Away from graves, and will do more of it."

That's how it is your wiser spirit speaks,
Rembrandt. If you believe him, why complain?
If not, why paint? And why, in any event,
305 Look back for the old joy and the old roses,
Or the old fame? They are all gone together,
And Saskia with them; and with her left out,
They would avail no more now than one strand
Of Samson's hair wound round his little finger
310 Before the temple fell. Nor more are you
In any sudden danger to forget
That in Apollo's house there are no clocks
Or calendars to say for you in time
How far you are away from Amsterdam,
315 Or that the one same law that bids you see
Where now you see alone forbids in turn
Your light from Holland eyes till Holland ears
Are told of it; for that way, my good fellow,
Is one way more to death. If at the first
320 Of your long turning, which may still be longer
Than even your faith has measured it, you sigh
For distant welcome that may not be seen,
Or wayside shouting that will not be heard,
You may as well accommodate your greatness
325 To the convenience of an easy ditch,
And, anchored there with all your widowed gold,
Forget your darkness in the dark, and hear
No longer the cold wash of Holland scorn.

HAUNTED HOUSE

Here was a place where none would ever come
For shelter, save as we did from the rain.
We saw no ghost, yet once outside again
Each wondered why the other should be dumb;
5   For we had fronted nothing worse than gloom
And ruin, and to our vision it was plain
Where thrift, outshivering fear, had let remain
Some chairs that were like skeletons of home.

There were no trackless footsteps on the floor
10   Above us, and there were no sounds elsewhere.
But there was more than sound; and there was more
Than just an axe that once was in the air
Between us and the chimney, long before
Our time. So townsmen said who found her there.

THE SHEAVES

Where long the shadows of the wind had rolled,
Green wheat was yielding to the change assigned;
And as by some vast magic undivined
The world was turning slowly into gold.
5   Like nothing that was ever bought or sold
It waited there, the body and the mind;
And with a mighty meaning of a kind
That tells the more the more it is not told.

So in a land where all days are not fair,
10   Fair days went on till on another day
A thousand golden sheaves were lying there,
Shining and still, but not for long to stay—
As if a thousand girls with golden hair
Might rise from where they slept and go away.

KARMA

Christmas was in the air and all was well
With him, but for a few confusing flaws
In divers of God's images. Because
A friend of his would neither buy nor sell,
5   Was he to answer for the axe that fell?
He pondered; and the reason for it was,
Partly, a slowly freezing Santa Claus
Upon the corner, with his beard and bell.

Acknowledging an improvident surprise,
10   He magnified a fancy that he wished
The friend whom he had wrecked were here again.
Not sure of that, he found a compromise;
And from the fulness of his heart he fished
A dime for Jesus who had died for men.

NEW ENGLAND

Here where the wind is always north-north-east
And children learn to walk on frozen toes,
Wonder begets an envy of all those
Who boil elsewhere with such a lyric yeast
5   Of love that you will hear them at a feast
Where demons would appeal for some repose,
Still clamoring where the chalice overflows
And crying wildest who have drunk the least.

Passion is here a soilure of the wits,
10   We're told, and Love a cross for them to bear;
Joy shivers in the corner where she knits
And Conscience always has the rocking-chair,
Cheerful as when she tortured into fits
The first cat that was ever killed by Care.

HECTOR KANE

If Hector Kane at eighty-five
Was not the youngest man alive,
Appearance had anointed him
    With undiminished youth.
5   To look at him was to believe
That as we ask we may receive,
Annoyed by no such evil whim
    As death, or time, or truth.

Which is to doubt, if any of you,
10 Seeing him, had believed him true.
He was too young to be so old,
    Too old to be so fair.
Beneath a snowy crown of curls,
His cheeks that might have been a girl's
15 Were certainly, if truth were told,
    Too rose-like to be there.

But Hector was a child of earth,
And would have held of little worth
Reflection or misgiving cast
20   On his reality.
It was a melancholy crime,
No less, to torture life with time;
And whoso did was first and last
    Creation's enemy.

He told us, one convivial night,
When younger men were not so bright
Or brisk as he, how he had spared
   His heart a world of pain,
Merely by seeing always clear
What most it was he wanted here,
And having it when most he cared,
   And having it again.

"You children of threescore or so,"
He said, "had best begin to know
If your infirmities that ache,
   Your lethargies and fears,
And doubts, are mostly more or less
Like things a drunkard in distress
May count with horror, while you shake
   For counting days and years.

"Nothing was ever true for me
Until I found it so," said he;
"So time for me has always been
   Four letters of a word.
Time? Is it anything to eat?
Or maybe it has legs and feet,
To go so as to be unseen;
   Or maybe it's a bird.

"Years? I have never seen such things.
Why let your fancy give them wings
To lift you from experience
   And carry you astray?
If only you will not be old,
Your mines will give you more than gold,
And for a cheerful diligence
   Will keep the worm away.

"We die of what we eat and drink,
But more we die of what we think;
For which you see me still as young
60   At heart as heretofore.
So here's to what's awaiting us—
Cras ingens iterabimus—"*
A clutch of wonder gripped his tongue,
And Hector said no more.

65   Serene and inarticulate
He lay, for us to contemplate.
The mortal trick, we all agreed,
    Was never better turned:
Bequeathing us to time and care,
70   He told us yet that we were there
To make as much as we could read
    Of all that he had learned.

---

* *"Cras ingens iterabimus aequor"* (Horace, *Odes* 1.7.32): "Tomorrow we will revisit the great sea." —Editor

FOR THE BEST IN PAPERBACKS, LOOK FOR THE

In every corner of the world, on every subject under the sun, Penguin represents quality and variety—the very best in publishing today.

For complete information about books available from Penguin—including Puffins, Penguin Classics, and Arkana—and how to order them, write to us at the appropriate address below. Please note that for copyright reasons the selection of books varies from country to country.

In the United Kingdom: Please write to *Dept. JC, Penguin Books Ltd, FREEPOST, West Drayton, Middlesex UB7 0BR.*

If you have any difficulty in obtaining a title, please send your order with the correct money, plus ten percent for postage and packaging, to *P.O. Box No. 11, West Drayton, Middlesex UB7 0BR*

In the United States: Please write to *Consumer Sales, Penguin USA, P.O. Box 999, Dept. 17109, Bergenfield, New Jersey 07621-0120.* Visa and MasterCard holders call 1-800-253-6476 to order all Penguin titles

In Canada: Please write to *Penguin Books Canada Ltd, 10 Alcorn Avenue, Suite 300, Toronto, Ontario M4V 3B2*

In Australia: Please write to *Penguin Books Australia Ltd, P.O. Box 257, Ringwood, Victoria 3134*

In New Zealand: Please write to *Penguin Books (NZ) Ltd, Private Bag 102902, North Shore Mail Centre, Auckland 10*

In India: Please write to *Penguin Books India Pvt Ltd, 706 Eros Apartments, 56 Nehru Place, New Delhi 110 019*

In the Netherlands: Please write to *Penguin Books Netherlands bv, Postbus 3507, NL-1001 AH Amsterdam*

In Germany: Please write to *Penguin Books Deutschland GmbH, Metzlerstrasse 26, 60594 Frankfurt am Main*

In Spain: Please write to *Penguin Books S.A., Bravo Murillo 19, 1° B, 28015 Madrid*

In Italy: Please write to *Penguin Italia s.r.l., Via Felice Casati 20, I-20124 Milano*

In France: Please write to *Penguin France S.A., 17 rue Lejeune, F-31000 Toulouse*

In Japan: Please write to *Penguin Books Japan, Ishikiribashi Building, 2-5-4, Suido, Bunkyo-ku, Tokyo 112*

In Greece: Please write to *Penguin Hellas Ltd, Dimocritou 3, GR-106 71 Athens*

In South Africa: Please write to *Longman Penguin Southern Africa (Pty) Ltd, Private Bag X08, Bertsham 2013*